Sports Law in South Africa

Sports Law in South Africa

Third Edition

Diederick Christoffel Jankowitz

This book was originally published as a monograph in the International Encyclopaedia of Laws/Sports Law.

Founding Editor: Roger Blanpain
General Editor: Frank Hendrickx
Volume Editor: Michele Colucci

Wolters Kluwer

Published by:
Kluwer Law International B.V.
PO Box 316
2400 AH Alphen aan den Rijn
The Netherlands
E-mail: international-sales@wolterskluwer.com
Website: lrus.wolterskluwer.com

Sold and distributed in North, Central and South America by:
Wolters Kluwer Legal & Regulatory U.S.
7201 McKinney Circle
Frederick, MD 21704
United States of America
Email: customer.service@wolterskluwer.com

Sold and distributed in all other countries by:
Air Business Subscriptions
Rockwood House
Haywards Heath
West Sussex
RH16 3DH
United Kingdom
Email: international-customerservice@wolterskluwer.com

ISBN 978-94-035-1944-9

e-Book: ISBN 978-94-035-1973-9
web-PDF: ISBN 978-94-035-1962-3

The Author

Diederick Christoffel Jankowitz completed his LLB at the North-West University's Potchefstroom Campus in South-Africa. He is an advocate of the High Court of South-Africa and a member of the South-African Society of Advocates. He completed various diplomas in international sports law and also a member of the *African Sports law & Business Journal*.

The Author wishes to thank Adv. Anton Alberts who assisted him in the writing of a more detailed discussion on the topic of politics in sports.

The Author

Table of Contents

Table of Contents

List of Abbreviations

ADR	Alternative Dispute Resolution
ASA	Advertising Standards Authority
ECA	Electronic Communications Act
ICASA	Independent Communications Authority of South Africa
IRB	International Rugby Board
IRT	Intermediary Regulation Tool
LAWSA	The Law of South-Africa
LRA	Labour Relations Act, Act 66 of 1999
NSRA	National Sport & Recreation Act, Act 110 of 1998
NSRP	National Sports and Recreation Plan
SAFA	South-African Football Association
SAFIA	South African Football Intermediary Association
SAFPU	South African Football Players Union
SAIDS	South-African Institute for Drugfree Sport
SANZAR	South-African, New-Zealand, Australian Rugby
SARPA	South-African Rugby Players Association
SARU	The South-African Rugby Union
SASC	South-African Sports Committee
SASCOC	South-African Sports Confederation and Olympic Committee
STP	Strategic Transformation Plan
TBCEA	The Basic Conditions and Employment Act, Act 75 of 1997
WADA	World Anti-doping Association

List of Abbreviations

General Introduction

Chapter 1. General Background

1. In order to understand sports law in South-Africa, one must, first of all, familiarize oneself with the South-African legal system.

§1. The South-African Legal System

2. The concept of the South-African legal system is the rule of law principal, which would mean that no person is punishable or can be lawfully made to suffer any damage without a breach of the law that applies to the ordinary courts of South-Africa. The concept also inclines that no person is above the law in South-Africa. On numerous occasions, the President of South-Africa had to appear in front of the High Court of South-Africa regarding disputes. A good example can be found in *SARFU and Others v. President of the Republic of South-Africa and Others 1998 (1) BCLR 1256 (T).*[1]

In South-Africa, the constitution provides that the Republic of South-Africa is one Sovereign democratic state founded on certain values which would include the supremacy of the constitution and the rule of law.[2]

The Bill of Rights, Chapter 2 of the Constitution is the cornerstone of the South-African democracy, and no law may be in conflict with this chapter. Hence, I do not want to bore the reader with a detailed discussion of the bill of rights; I will discuss the applicability of certain section in paragraphs following.[3]

§2. Making of Law in South-Africa

3. Broadly speaking in South-Africa, there are two ways of making law. By way of Legislation and the common law. The first mentioned is the declaration by a competent authority and the latter is the common law, which is based upon customs or is the result of judicial decisions.

1. *SARFU and Others v. President of the Republic of South-Africa and Others* 1998 (1) BCLR 1256 (T).
2. The Constitution of South Africa, Act 108 of 1996.
3. Act 108 of 1996 *supra.*

The Common law is based upon the Roman-Dutch law which is founded upon the law in Netherlands. This law developed through the centuries and was brought to South-Africa when Jan van Riebeeck landed on the coast of the Cape of Good Hope.

Chapter 2. Sources of Sports Law

4. Sport is subject to the laws of the country, whether statute or common law. In the South-African law history, one can find numerous examples of this. There existed old legislation that no sport may be played on Sundays.[4]

As sport becomes more and more commercialized and the financial burden that revolves around sport, the number of cases that revolves around sport is increasing by the minute, not only in South-Africa but also throughout the world.

The National Sport and recreation Act, Act 110 of 1998 aims to develop and promote recreation, equality and democracy in sport. The Act coordinates the relationships between the National Department of Sport and Recreation, also known as the sport and recreation South-Africa, and the Sports Confederation and other agencies.

The Act provides for measures aimed at correcting imbalances in sport and recreation, as well as an alternative dispute resolution ('ADR') mechanism to resolve disputes in sport. The act enables the minister of sport to put the necessary regulations and or policies in place.

The Minister of Sport and Recreation has the power to determine the general policy to be pursued with regard to sport and recreation.

In terms of the NSRA, the minister may adopt the said policy in relation to numerous matters which would include the roles and responsibilities of the various role-players in sport and recreation, the provision of funds for the building and upgrading of basic multipurpose sport and recreational facilities, the identifying of latent talent within the sport etc. The Sports-unification process as well as affirmative action measures, also known in South-Africa as transformation, to ensure that national teams would reflect all parties involved in the process, also form part of the said policy.

Initially, the South-African sports committee ('SASC') charged with the challenging task of promoting equity in sport, presenting mass sport participation programmes, addressing the shortage of trained leaders, administrators and officials at national level. I say this is a challenging task due to the multi-cultural society that exists in South-Africa. SASC was disestablished and the various tasks would now vest in the different national departments.

In allocating funds to national or recreational federations, the proportion of funding to be used towards development must be determined. No funds may be allocated to national and recreational federations where no development programmes exist or where certain persons from disadvantaged groups, especially women and people with disabilities, are excluded from participating at the top level of sport.

§1. Case Law

5. As mentioned earlier, the *stare decisis* principle forms a substantial part of the South-African legal system. It is integrated as such into the sports law of South Africa.

4. *Oehly and Others v. Rex* 1908.

§2. Rules of the Particular Game

6. It speaks for itself that the laws/rules of a specific sport would form an essential part of the sources of sports law with regards to the disciplinary process to be followed if the athlete breaches the laws of the game.

Chapter 3. Specificity of Sports

7. There exists no such thing as Sports law as a separate part in the South-African legal system, but have this 'umbrella term' evolved into a new legal area?

On this subject, divergent opinions have been expressed by writers.

Grayson said:[5] ' ... No subject exists which jurisprudentially can be called sports laws ... common law and equity create no concept of law relating exclusively to sport. Each area of law applicable to sport does not differ from how it is found in any other social or jurisprudential category.'

The Authors of Sports Law[6] said: 'The development of this subject area of law's involvement in sport is part of a process that has happened to all legal areas in the past. Labour or employment law is a subject area that has only achieved relatively recent recognition. It has its origins in contract in the employment context but no one would doubt that with the plethora of legislation regulating the workplace, it has become a subject area in its own right.'

At this point in time, in the South-African law concept, the term 'sports law' can be defined as an amalgamation of various legal disciplines encompassing sport. It would include various aspects of the law and can, therefore, be explained as any area of the law which would affect or be affected by sport. It is thus an umbrella term which embraces all the components of sport.[7]

In my opinion, the fact that sport as a whole transpired into one of the biggest forms of entertainment and that there exist certain topics such as 'game bonuses' that only exist in sports law would move me to be so bold to state that sports law as a separate legal area is a necessity.

Each sport has its set of rules that is considered to be part of a contract and can be legally enforced.

There are a few other sources of legislation that govern specific instances in sport. The South African Institute Free Drug Free Sport Act No. 17 of 1997 provides for doping control within the sport sphere. Boxing has its own act that governs the commercial boxing sector and so forth. I deal more thoroughly with each of these acts in the paragraphs following.

---

5. E. Grayson, *Sport & the Law*, 2nd ed, (Butterworthp 1994).
6. S. Gardiner, *Sports Law* (Cavendish Publishing 1998).
7. Law of South-Africa Vol. 8 2nd ed, Sports Law. Par 468.

Part I. Organization of Sport

Chapter 1. Sports Governance

8. Sport as a whole in South-Africa is being governed and regulated by the National Sport and Recreation Act, Act 110 of 1998.

For ease of reference, I quote the main part of the Act below:

> NATIONAL SPORT AND RECREATION ACT
> NO. 110 OF 1998
> National Sport and Recreation Amendment Act, No. 18 of 2007
> 2. Promotion and development of sport and recreation in Republic.–(1) The Minister must recognise in writing a Sports Confederation which will be the national co-ordinating macro body for the promotion and development of high performance sport in the Republic.
> [Sub-s. (1) substituted by s. 2 (a) of Act No. 18 of 2007.]
>
> (2) The Sports Confederation may, from time to time, develop guidelines for the promotion and development of high performance sport.
> [Sub-s. (2) substituted by s. 2 (b) of Act No. 18 of 2007.]
>
> (3) (a) Every government ministry, department, province or local authority may carry out sporting or recreational activities or activities relating to physical education, sport and recreation, including training programmes and development of leadership qualities.
> (b) In relation to high performance sport, a government ministry, department, province or local authority referred to in paragraph (a) may consult with the Sports Confederation.
> [Para. (b) substituted by s. 2 (c) of Act No. 18 of 2007.]
>
> (4) The Sports Confederation must co-ordinate all activities relating to high performance sport including team preparations and must consult with all the relevant sport bodies in that regard.
> [Sub-s. (4) substituted by s. 2 (d) of Act No. 18 of 2007.]
>
> (5) All national federations must develop its sports or recreational activity at club level in accordance with–
> a. the service level agreement referred to in section 3A;
> b. the development programmes referred to in section 10 (3); and

c. the guidelines issued by the Minister in terms of section 13A, and submit the progress on such development to Sport and Recreation South Africa and Parliament on an annual basis.

[Sub-s. (5) inserted by s. 2 (e) of Act No. 18 of 2007.]

(6) The Minister must advise the Minister of Finance if a national federation fails to develop its sports or recreational activity as contemplated in subsection (5), to be dealt with in accordance with an Act of Parliament administered by that Minister.

[Sub-s. (6) inserted by s. 2 (e) of Act No. 18 of 2007.]

3A. Service level agreement.–The Sports Confederation and national federations must, in the prescribed manner, enter into a service level agreement with Sport and Recreation South Africa in respect of any function assigned to them by this Act.

[S. 3A inserted by s. 4 of Act No. 18 of 2007.]

4. Determination of sport and recreation policy.–(1) The Minister may, after consultation with or after consideration of proposals made by the Sports Confederation in so far as high performance sport is concerned, from time to time, determine the general policy to be pursued with regard to sport and recreation.

[Sub-s. (1) substituted by s. 5 (a) of Act No. 18 of 2007.]

(2) The policy determined by the Minister may, among others, relate to the following:

a. Confirming the roles and responsibilities amongst the various role players in sport and recreation to ensure that all efforts are co-ordinated in an efficient manner;
b. providing funds annually for the creation and upgrading of basic multipurpose sport and recreation facilities subject to the provisions of section 10 and according to priorities as determined, from time to time, by Sport and Recreation South Africa in consultation with provincial and local government and relevant sport or recreation bodies;

   [Para. (b) substituted by s. 5 (b) of Act No. 18 of 2007.]
c. maintaining the focus on the administration of sport and recreation, as well as the development of a volunteer corps, to assist in the implementation of the various mass participation programmes;
d. enhancing health consciousness by means of themed programmes aimed at specific interest groups in the society;
e. identifying latent talent for sport;
f. investing in the preparation of sport participants who are elected to represent the Republic in major competitions;
g. helping in cementing the sports-unification process; and
h. instituting necessary affirmative action controls which will ensure that national teams reflect all parties involved in the process.

(3) The policy as determined by the Minister binds all sport or recreation bodies.

[Sub-s. (3) substituted by s. 5 (c) of Act No. 18 of 2007.]

5. …

[S. 5 deleted by s. 6 of Act No. 18 of 2007.]

6. National federations.–(1) National federations must assume full responsibility for the safety issues within their sport and recreation disciplines.
[Sub-s. (1) substituted by s. 7 (b) of Act No. 18 of 2007.]

(2) National federations must actively participate in and support programmes and services of Sport and Recreation South Africa and the Sports Confederation, in so far as high performance sport is concerned.
[Sub-s. (2) substituted by s. 7 (c) of Act No. 18 of 2007.]

(3) National federations must–
  a. before recruiting a foreign sport person to participate in sport in the Republic, satisfy themselves that there are no other persons in the Republic suitable to participate in such a sport;
  b. ensure that such a recruited sports person complies with all the relevant criteria pertaining to entry into the Republic as contemplated in the Immigration Act, 2002 (Act No 13 of 2002);
  c. advise the Minister in writing of the full names and countries of origin of all such persons recruited for such purposes and confirm that there are no other suitable persons in the Republic as contemplated in paragraph (a); and
  d. ensure that the recruitment conforms to the guidelines issued by the Minister in terms of section 13A.

[Sub-s. (3) inserted by s. 7 (d) of Act No. 18 of 2007.]

(4) For the purposes of this section, 'foreign sports person' means any person recruited in terms subsection (3) to participate in sport in the Republic including administrators or support staff.
[S. 6 amended by s. 7 (a) of Act No. 18 of 2007. Sub-s. (4) inserted by s. 7 (d) of Act No. 18 of 2007.]
7. Training of sport and recreation leaders.–

(1) The Sports Confederation may, in order to address the education and training needs in high performance sport:
  a. provide support in organising and presenting training workshops, courses and seminars for high performance sport leaders, managers, administrators, sport coaches and technical officials in cooperation with the relevant national federations and other macro-bodies;
  b. take steps to ensure that the training material is standardised in compliance with the unit standards as developed by the Standard Generating Bodies for Sport, Recreation and Fitness;
  c. maintain a database of trained high performance sport leaders, managers, administrators, sport coaches and technical officials referred to in paragraph (a) in cooperation with the relevant national federations and macro-bodies; and
  d. develop and continuously update a strategic framework for education and training.

(2) Sport and Recreation South Africa may, in order to address the education and training needs in sport and recreation:

a. provide support in organising and presenting training workshops, courses and seminars for sport and recreation leaders, managers, administrators, sport coaches and technical officials in cooperation with the relevant national federations and other macro-bodies;
b. take steps to ensure that the training material is standardised in compliance with the unit standards as developed by the Standard Generating Bodies for Sport, Recreation and Fitness;
c. maintain a database of trained sport and recreation leaders, managers, administrators, sport coaches and technical officials referred to in paragraph (a) in cooperation with the relevant national federations and macro-bodies; and
d. develop and continuously update a strategic framework for education and training.

[S. 7 substituted by s. 8 of Act No. 18 of 2007.]

Dispute resolution.–(1) (a) Every sport or recreation body must, in accordance with its internal procedure and remedies provided for in its constitution,_resolve any dispute arising among its members or with its governing body.

(b) The sport or recreation body must notify the Minister in writing of any dispute contemplated in paragraph (a) as soon it become aware of such dispute.

[Sub-s. (1) substituted by s. 13 (a) of Act No. 18 of 2007.]

(2) (a) Where the dispute cannot be resolved in terms of subsection (1), any member of the sport or recreation body in question who feels aggrieved, or the sport or recreation body itself, may submit the dispute to the Sports Confederation.
(b) The Sports Confederation must notify the Minister in writing of any dispute submitted to it in terms of paragraph (a).

[Sub-s. (2) substituted by s. 13 (b) of Act No. 18 of 2007.]

(3) The Sports Confederation must, in relation to any dispute referred to in subsection (1) or (2),–
a. notify the relevant parties of the allegations;
b. invite the parties to make representations to it;
c. convene where necessary an inquiry into the dispute; and
d. in accordance with the provisions of the Promotion of Administrative Justice Act, 2000 (Act No. 3 of 2000), notify the parties of the decision.

[Sub-s. (3) substituted by s. 13 (c) of Act No. 18 of 2007.]

(4) The Sports Confederation may, at any time, of its own accord, cause an investigation to be undertaken to ascertain the truth within a sport or recreation body, where allegations of–
a. any malpractice of any kind, including corruption, in the administration;

b. any serious or disruptive divisions between factions of the membership of the sport or recreation body; or
[Para. (b) substituted by s. 13 (e) of Act No. 18 of 2007.]

c. continuation or maintenance of any institutionalised system or practice of discrimination based on gender, race, religion or creed, or violation of the rights and freedoms of individuals or any law, have been made, and may ask the Minister to approach the President of the Republic to appoint a commission of inquiry referred to in section 84 (2)of the Constitution.

[Sub-s. (4) amended by s. 13 (d) of Act No. 18 of 2007.]

(5) (a) Subject to paragraph (b), the Minister may, after consultation with the relevant MEC if applicable, intervene–
- (i) in any dispute, alleged mismanagement, or any other related matter in sport or recreation that is likely to bring a sport or recreational activity into disrepute; or
- (ii) in any non compliance with guidelines or policies issued in terms of section 13A or any measures taken to protect or advance persons or categories of persons, disadvantaged by unfair discrimination as contemplated in section 9 (2) of the Constitution, by referring the matter for mediation or issuing a directive, as the case may be.

(b) The Minister may not–
- (i) intervene if the dispute or mismanagement in question has been referred to the Sports Confederation for resolution, unless the Sports Confederation fails to resolve such dispute within a reasonable time; and
- (ii) interfere in matters relating to the selection of teams, administration of sport and appointment of, or termination of the service of, the executive members of the sport or recreation body.

(c) If a national federation fails to adhere to a decision of the mediator or directive issued by the Minister as referred to paragraph (a), the Minister may–
- (i) direct Sport and Recreation South Africa to refrain from funding such federation;
- (ii) notify the national federation in writing that it will not be recognised by Sport and Recreation South Africa; and
- (iii) publish his or her decision as contemplated in subparagraphs (i) and (ii) in the Gazette.

9. This Act came about after the disestablishment of the National Sports Commission. The last-mentioned commission was disestablished by the National Sports Commission Amendment Act, 18 of 2007.

In terms of the Act, the minister must recognize a so-called sports confederation. All of the different sport federations must conclude a service level agreement with the sports confederation and must conduct business in terms hereof.

The sport federations are bound by the Service Level Agreement and by the Act and must develop its sports or recreational activity in accordance with the guidelines and development programmes as issued by the minister from time to time.

When determining a policy, the minister must consult with the confederation where after it can determine the policy, the last-mentioned may relate to the following aspects, confirmation of the roles and responsibilities of the various role players within the sport law, the provision of annual funds for the creation and upgrading of basic multipurpose sport and recreation facilities, retaining the focus on sport, enhancement of health consciousness, identifying latent talent, investing in preparation of sport participants, helping with the sport unification process and instituting the necessary affirmative action regulations.

The different national federations, which would include the different sport clubs must ensure as far as practicable the safety of the sport and must further ensure that a South-African citizen receives preference for a specific position above a player from a different nationality (foreign player).

With regards to ADR, the NSRA provides for a procedure in an attempt to resolve disputes as economic and cost-effective as possible. Each sport must attempt to resolve any dispute internally in accordance with its constitution.

Each sport has its own set of rules to take into account when resolving disputes internally.

Boxing in turn have its own Act, the South African Boxing Act[8] that aims to provide a new structure for professional boxing in the Republic, to ensure the effective and efficient administration of professional boxing in the Republic, to recognize amateur boxing, to create synergy between professional and amateur boxing, to establish a Boxing Commission known as Boxing SA, to promote interaction between associations of boxers, managers, promoters, trainers and officials and Boxing SA, and to provide for matters connected therewith.[9]

If a dispute cannot be resolved internally with the use of the aforementioned, the aggrieved party may refer the matter to the Confederation. The Confederation may order to investigate a specific incident. If it still cannot be resolved, the aggrieved party may refer it to the applicable court.

Even though the above process is stipulating that a party may refer a matter to the Confederation, the party may proceed to the applicable court with jurisdiction as well.

Most of the different sports' constitution makes reference to the Court of Arbitration of sport and the last-mentioned may resolve different disputes within the sports law.

---

8. Act 11 of 2001 on Boxing, LAWSA Vol. 8 2nd ed, Entertainment & sportslaw.
9. Act 11 of 2001 *supra,* LAWSA Vol. 8 2nd ed, Entertainment & sportslaw.

§1. NATIONAL OLYMPIC COMMITTEE AND SPORT ASSOCIATIONS

10. If one reads the Act, it seems that the Olympic Committee and the confederation are two separate entities, but in practice, they are in fact one and the same body. The sports body is known as SASCOC, the South-African sports confederation and Olympic committee.

In terms of the Sport and Recreation Act, the Confederation (SASCOC) has certain duties to perform to enable enforcement of said act. This has to be done in order to facilitate the governance of sport in South-Africa.

Chapter 2. Public Regulation

§1. Fundamental Rights

I. Freedom of Association

11. In South-Africa, the Bill of Rights,[10] Chapter 2 of the constitution, determines the fundamental rights of each person. The Bill of Rights is superior to all of the other legislation and if legislation contains any regulation contradicting the *Bill of Rights* it is considered to be unconstitutional and therefore invalid. I am only going to discuss the most relevant sections to sports law in the Bill of Rights in South-Africa.

Section 18 of the Constitution determines the following: 'Everybody has the right to freedom of association.'

The right protects contact with others and cooperation for joint purposes. It is an important right because an individual can exercise and protect his or her other individual rights more effectively in cooperation with others. The right protects an individual's freedom to form and join associations and to participate in their activities and the freedom of associations to pursue their goals freely. Certain forms of free association are guaranteed in other provisions of the Bill of Rights, for example, in respect of political parties, trade unions and employers' organizations and cultural, religious and linguistic associations.

In the South-African context, this section is not as straightforward as it seems; there are limitations to this right which I would discuss fully in the paragraphs following.

One must start at the beginning and first determine what exactly is contained in the section.

More than a century ago, Alexis de Toque wrote that no one especially no legislator can attack the freedom of association without impairing the very limits of society.[11]

According to another writer, Waltzer, if we continue to ignore the foundational nature of associations, we do so at our own peril.

The South-African civil society was a palpably thin affair during the previous regime. And certain cornerstones, which I would discuss underneath, had to be taken into account when referring to this right.[12]

II. Associations as Correlative

12. Freedom of association buttresses, makes well, the promise of a variety of other rights. Association understood in this context is a correlative right. The right to associate with whomever one deems fit enable a self-understanding that the state cannot determine who can be loved and how must they be loved.

10. The Constitution of South-Africa, Act 108 of 1996.
11. A. De Tocqueville, *Democracy in America*, 1st ed, 222 (1835).
12. Curie & De Waal, *The Bill of Rights Handbook*, 5th ed, 422 & 423.

III. Associations as Constitutive

13. 'Freedom of association rightly understood forces us to the rationality of our most basic attachments and to think twice before we accord our rational attachments preferred status to the rational attachments of others.'[13]

IV. Associations and Capture

14. The structure of associations is worth protecting. Associations may control their members by way of selective membership, selecting members within certain criteria. This process is called capture. The capture element is very important to protect the Association. If the association cannot determine who its members can be, it will obviously derail the purpose of the association. It would also be easy to get access to the association and the association can then be damaged by 'uninvited members'.

V. Associations and Disassociation

15. It speaks for itself that when a person has the right to associate, he would also receive the right to disassociate.

The South-African legal system makes provision therefore that certain forms of associations would not receive any protection. These forms, although few and far between, would more or less constitute any unlawful associations for instance gangs or any form of criminal associations.

As a result of South-Africa's chequered past, the constitution provides for a section that any right may be limited.[14] This would include the right of freedom of association. The section reads as follows:

Limitation of rights

1. The rights in the Bill of rights may be limited only in terms of law of general application to the extent that the limitation is reasonable and justifiable in an open and democratic society based on human dignity, equality and freedom, taking into account all relevant factors, including-
   a. The nature of the right;
   b. The importance of the purpose of the limitation
   c. The nature or extent of the limitation;
   d. The relation between the limitation and its purpose; and
   e. Less restrictive means to achieve the purpose.
2. Except as provided in subsection (1) or any other provision of the Constitution, no law may limit any right entrenched in the bill of rights.

13. The Bill of rights handbook, *supra.*
14. Section 36 of act 108 of 1996 *supra.*

In the aforementioned, it can be seen that the right of freedom of association can also be limited. The intervention of the state would more likely take one of the following forms: (1) banning, (2) a forced change in entrance and voice consistent with the dictates of equality, (3) requiring the internal organization of the association to conform to basic democratic principles and (4) an attempt to prevent undue coercion.[15]

VI. Banning

16. This ground for interference is more or less banning of certain criminal associations. These associations will not receive protection whatsoever from the state.

A forced change in entrance and voice consistent with the *Dictates of* Equality.

In South-Africa, the promotion of Equality and Prevention of Unfair discrimination *Act 4 of 2000*[16] provides that certain associations must open themselves for a wider range in potential members. It goes even further than that and makes equality per se an overriding principle.

VII. Democracy

17. The state may interfere and put certain measures in place to prevent any association to disturb the democratic society.

VIII. Coercion

18. The difficulty in this ground lays with being in a world that radically constrains on how individuals act.

I am not going to go into detail hereof as this ground is in my opinion not relevant to the sports law of South-Africa.

IX. Freedom of Association and the Sports Law

19. This is directly relevant to the sports law as it will include most of the sport bodies such as football clubs, rugby clubs etc.

One has the right to associate with whichever club they want to.

The sports bodies, sports clubs, would receive protection from the state. There exists actually one perquisite before they would be protected; they would have to be acceptable in an open and democratic society.

15. Bill of Rights Handbook *supra.*
16. The Promotion of Equality and Prevention of Unfair Discrimination Act 4 of 2000.

As explained previously to be acceptable in an open and democratic society, no unfair discrimination may exist. Equality must be promoted as prescribed by numerous laws in South-Africa. This is done to level the proverbially playing field for each person in South-Africa.

This would include the different quota systems in the different sports. There is actually no such thing as transformation in our laws, but this is the new terminology used to describe said system in sport.

I will discuss the last-mentioned issue, with the assistance of Adv. Anton Alberts, in §2 underneath.

§2. Quota System in South-African Sport

20. Different sports in South-Africa have different quota systems. I would discuss the quota systems in the three national sports (Rugby union, Cricket, Football) of South-Africa in the paragraphs following:

I. Rugby Union

21. South-Africa is currently ranked 5th in the world. The Government of South-Africa implemented certain quota systems as they are of the opinion that the South-African Rugby union sides are not a positive representation of the diverse cultures of the Nation.

The South-African rugby union, SARU, adopted a so-called strategic transformation plan ('STP'). This plan is again like many other laws in the country solely based on racial terms:

1. It is first of all important to a few definitions contained in the STP:
   - Generic Black people are defined as black African, Coloured and Indian people.
   - Black African is not specifically defined but is generally understood to mean a South-African of an indigenous African tribe.

The STP has set a target that at least 50% of a team have to be represented by generic black players before such a team can be regarded as transformed.

In terms of the STP, it is a requirement that by the year 2019 all of the teams competing within one of South-Africa's national competitions have to be generic black.

At this point in time, the quota system for the national competitions is as follows:

> The government set a 2019 target for rugby by which time 50% of the teams must be Black. This action is in line with the ANC-government's 'Transformation' and 'representivity' logic, despite utterances that no racial quotas exist. According to reports the sport is on target but this will be seen in September 2019 during the rugby world cup.

II. Cricket

22. South-Africa is ranked 4th in the world on test level as well as on the One Day International stage. On the T20 stage, South-Africa is being ranked 6th in the World.

At this point in time, the quota system for the Provincial cricket in the National competitions is as follows:

> six black players per franchise team (of which at least 3 must be ethnically Black).

III. Football

23. On the World stage, South-Africa is ranked 73rd. There exists no quota system in football. It is the opinion of the government that the football teams are fully representative of the South-African diverse nation.

§3. Sport and Politics

24. South Africa is by any measure a very successful sporting nation that has produced some of the greatest athletes and sports teams in the world before and after the political transition in 1994. Since South Africa's political transition, the new government has taken it upon itself, being a progressive force, to ensure that equity takes a front seat in sport. This means that the ANC-government tried to ensure through its policies and laws that sport would develop into a fair playing ground where all South-Africans will have access to participate in any sport of their choosing and that sport becomes an instrument of nation-building. In this regard, it is quite apt to quote President Nelson Mandela from his speech given at the Laureus World Sports Awards Ceremony in 2000 – and to be used as a measure of government policies, laws and action:[17]

> Sport has the power to change the world. It has the power to inspire. It has the power to unite people in a way that little else can. Sport can awake hope where there was previously only despair.

Having said this it is also of grave importance to note that any intervention by a government in an aspect of the social domain of humans can go too far and/or can have negative consequences, both foreseeable and unforeseen. This introduction will cast a brief view on the current government's interventionist policies, laws and actions with regard to sport development and management in South Africa and will address the consequences thereof.

17. This was quotation was taken from the cover of the Department of Sport and Recreation's publication of the National Sport and Recreational Plan.

25. The starting point in comprehending the government's stance on sport itself is to analyse the ANC-government's general view regarding equity and redress. The ANC's central view has always been that the wrongs of the past must be addressed in an affirmative manner. Thus, the patterns from the past must be changed by making use of governmental power. The effect thereof is that the state assumes a very overt progressive and interventionist role in the affairs of South-Africans. According to this world view, there cannot be equity and therefore no justice without the state, spearheaded by the legislative and executive branches of the state, but especially the executive, in the form of policies, laws and enforcement. Natural civic compliance based on national consensus takes a back seat in accordance with this world view, although this also plays a role – but as will be seen, a very subdued one easily replaced by state enforcement when the government does not get what it wants.

The ANC-government's world view is titled 'Transformation' and has taken on a very specific form over and above its normal semantic meaning. In essence, it is based on the demographic reality of post-apartheid South Africa and acts as an ideological counterweight to the ideology of apartheid itself. As apartheid divided people based on race and to a degree also ethnicity, the counterweight to this is to ensure that logically no divisions exist and that the black majority that was excluded before, is now the beneficiary of opportunity as well, with an added benefit based on redress. This position is, however, further complemented with a major idea that ironically sounds and works in practice as the flipside side of the coin of apartheid, namely representivity.

The term 'representivity' forms the essence of the ethos of 'Transformation'. It basically entails that every facet of the social sphere in the country must be 'transformed' to be representative of the demographics of the country. In practice, it means that all walks of life shall be dominated by the black majority with the minorities in the form of whites, Coloureds and Indians, taking a back seat based on their inferior numbers. Thus the ANC-government has already, based on this logic, successfully transformed many spheres of life, such as the civil service that is currently over-representative of blacks in terms of the people employed. The logic of 'representivity' is also importantly inclusive of 'over-representivity' by the demographically dominant group as the ANC-government finds it acceptable that the black group can exceed the demographic quota and does, therefore, have no political will to at the very least keep to their own designed quota system of representivity, as long as it is at the expense of the minority group and not the majority. As will be explained later, this logic is also evident in the social sphere of sport.

South Africa is a constitutional democracy. Its Bill of Rights in Chapter 2 of the Constitution mandates compliance to and respect for certain rights by the state towards the individual on a vertical level – as well as groups in some cases – and the same relations between individuals on a horizontal level – as well as groups in certain cases. Given this dynamic, the ANC-government is obliged to base its interventionist logic of 'Transformation' and 'representivity' on a Constitutional rule.

This rule is found in section 9 of the Constitution that contains the equality clause. The basic point of departure is that everyone is equal before the law and entitled to equal protection and benefit of the law. There exists, however, an exception to the baseline rule, and that is that equality may be promoted by legislative and other measures 'designed to protect or advance persons, or categories of persons, disadvantaged by unfair discrimination … '.[18] This means that intervention can legally take place in order to ensure equity for those persons that were disadvantaged by unfair discrimination and it is upon this rule that the ANC-government has cemented its 'Transformation' and 'representivity'-logic.[19]

This equality exception rule has given rise to a whole spate of legislative interventions in the fields of employment and labour,[20] business,[21] government procurement,[22] and not least sport itself.

26. By the logic of 'representivity', all sports team must reflect the demographic reality of the South-African population. This implies the setting of a racial quota. In fulfilling this objective, the ANC-government created a Department of Sport and Recreation and empowered it to take charge of all national sport by virtue of the National Sport and Recreation Act 110 of 1998 (as amended).[23] More specifically the Department of Sport, designed the National Sports and Recreation Plan ('NSRP') that arose from a National Sports Indaba held in November 2011.[24]

The NRSP's twin mandate is to create an active and winning nation. The Minister of Sport and Recreation, Mr Fikile Mbalula, stated the objectives of the NRSP as follows:[25] 'We would like to see a community where at least 50% of all South-Africans participate in sport or active recreation; and where there is sustainable talent identification, nurturing and development programmes in place that contribute to transforming the demographic of the sports sector.'

27. The Minister continues to embed the whole NRSP's logic in the 'Transformation' worldview:[26]

---

18. Section 9(2) of the South African Constitution.
19. It deserves to be emphasized that section 9(2) of the Constitution is merely an exception to the equality rule, and this is further underscored by section 9(3) that states that the 'state may not unfairly discriminate directly or indirectly against anyone' amongst others on race, and section 9(5) that states that any discrimination on any of the grounds listed in section 9(3) is considered 'unfair unless it is established that the discrimination is fair'.
20. Witness the Employment Equity Act 55 of 1998. Interesting enough, the courts have confirmed that the setting of racial quotas in terms of this Act is not permissible.
21. Witness the Broad-Based Black Economic Empowerment Act 53 of 2003 and its various Codes of Good Practice in generic form and per certain industry. In terms of the generic Codes, it is permissible for a business to be 100% black and even preferable (and thus 'over-representative') as it will garner maximum points towards its BBBEE status for trading purposes, while a 100% white-owned business will be heavily penalized and effectively excluded from the trading system by way of a negative rating.
22. Witness the Preferential Procurement Policy Framework Act 5 of 2000 and its regulations.
23. By virtue of this Act, the government has created a connection between itself and the various voluntary sports bodies in the country and has confirmed its rights to confer national colours and allow international sporting events to take place.
24. The NSRP is a consensus document approved at the National Sport and Recreation Indaba and signed by all major role players in the sports domain. Hereby the ANC-government has ensured the cooperation of all major sports bodies to implement race-based selection policies without enacting an enforcing law.
25. Page 3 of the National Sport and Recreational Plan.
26. *See* page 4 of the National Sport and Recreational Plan (NSRP).

> It is for this reason that at the core of the NRSP is a Transformation Charter whose purpose is to transform the delivery of sport in South Africa and to reap such benefits as the establishment of a competitive and *demographically representative* sports system. (Emphasis added)

The NSRP spells out a broad and grand vision for South African sports for the year 2030.[27] One of its goals is to achieve transformation by that date.

The debate that is currently taking place with regard to the ANC-government's sports plans is whether it will actually work as envisaged and whether, from the minorities' point of view, the NSRP does not in some way exceed the provisions of section 9 of the Constitution by turning section 9(2) into the norm replacing the apex norm of equality. Numerous examples can be cited where minority players have felt aggrieved for not been chosen to a team or for a tournament purely based on the colour of their skin, as it would interfere with the racial targets. Even on school level, many talented white players have been side-lined due to the quota system and some of those parents have decided to immigrate to rugby countries, like Australia, where discrimination based on race does not take place. Quotas also have a reverse negative effect on Black players as they are labelled as 'quota players' no matter how well they may perform.[28]

28. In practice, the government and sports bodies argue that no racial quotas are being set, yet the practices and rhetoric of the government paints a different picture. The Minister of Sport and Recreation recently commanded the five major sports bodies[29] to increase their 'Transformation' initiatives more aggressively and informed their respective sporting bodies that they will not be allowed to host future international events in South Africa unless they meet their 'Transformation' targets. The Minister, amongst others, set a 2019 target for rugby by which time 50% of the teams must be Black. This action is in line with the ANC-government's 'Transformation' and 'representivity' logic, despite utterances that no racial quotas exist. While the Minister states that he allows sports bodies to make their own decisions on 'Transformation', the pressure applied by government to introduce Black players into teams has resulted in sports bodies initiating quota systems that has started to result in the decay of social cohesion. The press reported in January 2016 how White players were on the verge of boycotting provincial cricket if the quota-rule of six Black players per franchise team (of which at least three must be ethnically Black) imposed by Cricket SA is not relaxed.[30] The ability of sport to unite a racially and ethnically diverse South-African community, as envisaged by Nelson Mandela, is ironically not coming to fruition as yet and might never.

The arguments for or against or even for a measured approach to 'Transformation' has resulted in the pitting of the ideas of equity and merit against each other and on a broader scale pitting the notions of normalizing South-Africa against that

27. *See* page 15 of the NSRP.
28. *See* http://mg.co.za/article/2014-09-11-black-players-conflicted-over-new-csa-quotas.
29. The five major sport types that are especially targeted for 'Transformation' is rugby, soccer, athletics, cricket and netball.
30. https://www.enca.com/sport/concerns-over-crickets-new-quota-system.

of the re-racialization of the country against each other. Interestingly, in a recent poll, it was found that most South-Africans prefer that the best person be given a job irrespective of race.[31] This can be extrapolated to the sports domain as well.

Despite differences in approaches to create equal opportunities for all South-Africans to access sport, there seems to be a broad consensus that development is the key. However, there is unfortunately a great divergence in thinking on what development means. The ANC-government supports a view of equal outcomes which translates into goals or quotas that must be met at certain milestones that inevitably negate merit – which is the central ethos of sports – and those opposed to this view supports development based on equal opportunity to participate in sports and develop their talents over time.

29. The Transformation Charter[32] in the NSRP, that binds South-African sports bodies to 'Transformation', sets out a scorecard with seven dimensions of which demography is only one, but in reality, the demographic theme has twisted its way into the other dimensions as well. An analysis of all seven dimensions and government practice are quite instructive in how race-based goals – and thus the idea of equal outcomes – permeates the whole government scheme:

- *Access:* Measures, amongst others, sports participants in general, sports participants in primary and secondary schools, participants between 18 and 21 years, number of affiliated clubs, operational clubs in each province, the number of operational facilities, the percentage of sports facilities accessible by sports persons with disabilities. While government funding to create access to all, especially in poor communities, is a sensible approach to create opportunities for development, the NSRP ironically states explicitly that this measurement relates to demographic change and 'Black representation'.[33] Despite the ANC-government arguing that 'Transformation' is, amongst others, based on the Founding Values of non-racialism found in the Constitution, race is the central theme in the government's 'Transformation'-ethos. These types of internal contradictions permeate ANC-government policy. Access would thus mean that facilities must be created for Blacks only and that, for instance, poor White communities will never be afforded any sports facilities. The NRSP is clear that there is a blanket ban on the creation of access for poor Whites, placing a serious question mark on the ANC-government's notion of equality and social justice. It is, therefore, ironic that the government has thus far failed to facilitate the development and maintenance of sports facilities in poor Black communities.[34]

---

31. For a full report and discussion of the poll as it relates to BEE, *see* the following link: http://irr.org.za/reports-and-publications/atLiberty/files/liberty-2013-bee-doesnt-work-but-eed-would.
32. The NSRP states on page 85 that the concept of transformation has its foundation in the Constitution with four distinct parts of the Constitution that 'set the tone, the parameters and the rationale for transformation … '. Those parts are: (1) the Preamble of the Constitution; (2) the Founding Values of the Constitution; (3) the Equality Clause of the Bill of Rights; and (4) the Human Dignity Clause of the Bill of Rights.
33. *See* page 96 of the NSRP.
34. The Department of Sport and Recreation's Annual Performance Plan for 2016/2017 (page 56) states that the Department to date does not know how many sport and recreational facilities exist and where

- *Skill and Capacity Development:* Measures various training outcomes, such as new accredited courses, and accredited administrators, technical officials and coaches trained on a national and international level.
- *Demographic Dimension:* Measures representation of Black people, females and people with disabilities in management, accredited coaching, and referee/umpire positions on national and provincial levels. Further measures Black people in senior and junior teams on national and provincial levels, as well as the percentage of participants who are female and people with disabilities at national and provincial levels. The racial dimension is hereby introduced and as can be witnessed, is measured across the whole sporting domain despite being only one of the 'dimensions' of measurement in the Transformation Scorecard. This outcome is confirmed in the NSRP's stated objective of the demographic dimension: 'Ensure the establishment of a sustainable pipeline of sport participants and supporters by changing sport's demographic profile on and off the field of play so that it reflects regional and local population demographics.'[35] Interestingly the NSRP states further that school sport development has to be a key focus area thereby bringing the equal opportunity logic into the mix instead of the equal outcomes ideology. However, as stated before, this is not what is taking place in practice as quota outcomes are explicitly expected from government while the development of school sport in poorer communities is not taking place. Furthermore, it is also quite clear that 'over-representivity' is also not regarded as a breach of equity as the national soccer team regularly fields a 100% Black team in international tournaments. On the flipside fielding, a 100% White team in any sport would be regarded as a cardinal sin. The implication is that a South African society completely dominated by Blacks at the complete exclusion of minorities is a measure of 'normal' for the ANC-government.
- *Performance:* This dimension relates to achievement and measures the number of recognised international competitions participating in, world ranking for team sports and the number of athletes ranked in top 20 positions in individual sports, the percentage of representative participants in High-Performance Programmes, and the number of officials serving on recognized international panels. This dimension represents the essence of sport, namely achievement. South Africa has a proud record of sporting achievements, yet overall a serious decline in quality of play is being witnessed. This dimension stands diametrically opposed to the notion of racial quotas and its weighting in practice within the overall scorecard is to be placed in serious question. Numerous examples exist of coaches in rugby, cricket, and netball being forced to field players not in top playing form merely to meet racial targets. It is very clear that the demographic dimension has a greater status within the overall Transformation Scorecard with an insidious influence on all other dimensions, especially the Performance dimension. This is

---

they are based in the country and that an accurate audit is absent due to the cost involved. This means that the Department is flying blind in the provision of access (operational facilities) as per its own NSRP Plan and further acknowledges that it is now providing infrastructure on an ad hoc basis. This is a material failure by the Department itself to set infrastructure targets, implement infrastructure plans and to measure its own success or lack thereof.

35. *See* page 101 of the NSRP.

not to imply there no good and great Black sportsmen- and women, but that there are not enough of them and that development should actually take centre-stage instead of quotas.

- *Contribution to Government Priorities:* Measures the number of programmes in support of HIV and AIDS, awareness programmes in support of sport and environment, social cohesion, sport for peace and development, job creation, sport against crime, and the percentage of procurement of enterprises that are BEE compliant. While this dimension has laudable objectives it is unfortunately in several aspects closely tied to the ANC-government's 'Transformation' ideas. In this regard, the BEE procurement indicator is subject to the Broad-Based Black Economic Empowerment Act and its various Codes of Good Practice that has been sharpened to now even exclude the awarding of BEE points to businesses for employing White females and people with disabilities. Previously the two aforementioned groups were included in the ranks of the employable designated groups for which businesses could score BBBEE points to enhance their status for government and big business procurement opportunities.[36] The effect of this change is that any business operating in the sports domain and employing any White females or people with disabilities will be penalised for employing them by achieving a lower BBBEE score and will, based on the NSRP Transformation Scorecard, not be a very suitable business to consider for procurement purposes. The theme of racial social engineering is thus running strongly as a golden thread throughout the NSRP dimensions and interacting with the greater matrix of race-based legislation[37] to ensure a comprehensive governmental regime of 'Transformation'.
- *Good Governance:* Measures compliance to the King III Report on good governance in general and adds to this the 'Transformation' aspects of 'selection policy' that will inevitably be influenced by the racial demographic dimension, and 'inputs made in realising the National Sports and Recreation Plan' of which the objective is changing sport to reflect the demographic reality of the country. Good governance has thus become another measuring device to ensure compliance with racial policies.
- *Overall Transformation Scorecard:* Combines all of the previous six dimensions into one scorecard to measure the achievement of each dimension and all of them collectively. Having regard to the above analysis of the theory and practice of the dimensions, a general racial theme based on quotas is evident. Even where the

36. The ANC-government's reaction to the slow pace of 'Transformation' is to sharpen it even more while abundant evidence exists that race-based economic intervention is simply not working and actually slowing the economy down by placing an unnecessary burden on business. During the public hearings and deliberations on the Broad-Based Black Economic Empowerment Amendment Bill of 2012 the author of the original BBEEE idea that led to the creation of the Act, the Rothchilds Consultancy, clearly indicated that BBBEE is not working and that we should go back to the drawing board. Dr Anthea Jeffery, Head of Policy Research at the Institute of Race Relations, also authored a book 'BEE – helping or hurting?' outlining the nature of BEE in all social spheres and the cost of it on the economy and poverty reduction. *See* the following link for more information: http://irr.org.za/reports-and-publications/atLiberty/files/liberty-2013-bee-doesnt-work-but-eed-would.
37. Especially the Broad-Based Black Economic Empowerment Act 53 of 2003 and the Employment Equity Act 55 of 1998.

NSRP Transformation Scorecard emphasises development (to create equal opportunities) in relation to the Demographic Dimension, practice by government and sports bodies contradict this logic by imposing racial quotas either directly or by stealth.[38]

30. Each of the dimensions consists of columns that require the setting of targets, actual achievement measurement and a score. There must thus be no illusion about the nature of the NSRP Transformation Scorecard: compliance must be achieved.

In conclusion, a clear picture emerges of the ANC-government interfering in South-African sports by making use of legal and moral instruments as follows:

- *The National Sports and Recreation Act 110 of 1998:* whereby the government and specifically the Minister can deny sporting bodies' national accreditation, national sport colours to athletes and allow or ban major international sporting events.
- *The National Sport and Recreation Plan:* whereby the government has morally bound the major sport bodies to participate in 'Transformation' and the setting of targets which merely serves as code for racial quotas. Targets are set and must be complied with at the whim of the Minister who can use the above-mentioned Act to enforce compliance.

31. A Constitutional analysis that could answer the lingering question whether the ANC-government's use of section 9(2) equality exception rule violates the apex equality rule in section 9(1), can possibly be answered by having regard to Labour Law. If one accepts that sportsmen and women are employees, then the differentiation made between numerical targets and quotas made by the Constitutional Court in the case of *Solidarity and Others v. Department of Correctional Services and Others* SA 594 (CC) (15 July 2016) is quite apt. The Constitutional Court confirmed that numerical targets are flexible goals where discretion based on factors other than race and gender for selection and appointment still plays a role. Quota, however, is inflexible and places a bar on any discretion to change selection and appointment and effectively 'operates as an absolute barrier to the appointment of some … ' based on race and gender.

Within this Labour Law context should the ANC-government and the sports bodies at any point view the targets in the NSRP Transformation Scorecard as fixed, they will be quotas and illegal. The fact that the Minister imposes racial objectives upon sporting bodies against the threat of Ministerial sanctions and the sporting bodies in turn reserve definitive positions in sport teams looks sinisterly like job reservation based on race, and thus unconstitutional.

32. The ANC-government's interference in sport by imposing on it its objective of a South-Africa that reflects the demography is an example of how government is

38. *See* the following article on the conflicting views of Cricket SA whether they have been implementing quotas in the national cricket team all along (while denying it) or has only explicitly started now: http://mg.co.za/article/2014-09-11-black-players-conflicted-over-new-csa-quotas.

intervening in all spheres of life. The effect of 'Transformation' in the economic sphere is even more devastating in nature.

South-Africans of all walks of life deserve sport opportunities and paths that can lead to excellence. Development interventions in the NSRP Transformation Scorecard that focus on the dimensions of access, skills development and performance within a social environment where employment creating and poverty-reducing economic growth takes place is the proven solution to establish equity and redress without falling back on the markers of race. The ANC-government understands this, but racial politics has thus far ensured it successive electoral successes. This strategy will not last for long as is evidenced by the electoral growth of the opposition during the 2014 and 2016 elections. In the meantime, South African sport is mired, like much of South African society at large, in the muddy politics of race.

§4. Civil Liability

33. Civil law concerns the adjudication upon and settling of disputes between citizens or a dispute between a citizen and the state, like refer to previously herein.

Each person has fundamental rights, and if there is an infringement on one of these rights a dispute will arise whether the dispute is with regard to a contract or with regard to a delict, tort.

Certain delictual acts would also be considered as criminal activities; therefore, it is possible for a person to be sued out of the civil court and be charged with a criminal offence as well.

Delict

34. As a small introduction to the law of delict in South-Africa, I would like to quote the following passage from The Law of South-Africa.[39] The essential characteristic of the South-African law of delict is that it is founded on general principles of liability. This is the product of a long historical evolution. In this respect, it differs fundamentally from the English law of torts which, despite the unifying force and influence of the concept of negligence, is still basically a casuistic system. The South-African law of delict is therefore not a random collection of miscellaneous, unrelated wrongs, but a detailed body of principles, rules and concepts founded on historically developed broad bases of liability. In this respect, it bears a certain resemblance to the Continental systems of law which developed from the same historical sources. The influence of English law has not changed or replaced the basic foundations of the law of delict. Although English law has certainly contributed to the superstructure of the South-African law of delict, it is still founded on the principles and concepts of Roman and Roman-Dutch law.

However, the common law principles are not to remain static. The Constitution enjoins courts to develop the common law according to the values enshrined in the Bill of Rights. It is the supreme law, and common law principles must be reassessed

---

39. Midgley & Van Der Walt, LAWSA Vol. 8(1) 2nd ed, para. 23.

to bring them into line with its provisions. How this is to be done is discussed elsewhere. Suffice it to note here that the norms and values enshrined in the Constitution, and developed by the Constitutional Court, now serve not only as a yardstick for determining whether old principles are still current but also as a source and inspiration for developing new principles and rules. To that extent, the Bill of Rights can now be considered as the fourth pillar upon which our law of delict rests – together with the *lex Aquilia*, the *actio iniuriarum* and the remedy for pain and suffering.

The general basis and approach of South African law has been formulated as follows in *Perlman v. Zoutendyk*: 'Roman Dutch Law approaches a new problem in the continental rather than the English way, because in general all damage caused unjustifiably (injuria) is actionable, whether caused intentionally (dolo) or by negligence (culpa).'

35. In general, therefore, the South African law of delict is founded on the basic principle that all harm caused by wrongful and blameworthy (or culpable) conduct can be recovered by delictual action. To claim compensation in respect of patrimonial loss, for example, a plaintiff must show that he or she sustained harm (damnum), which was wrongfully and culpably (iniuria) caused (datum) by the defendant, while an iniuria is the wrongful and intentional infringement of an interest of personality.

The broad bases of the law of delict provide elastic and adaptable principles of liability for application to novel situations. However, the inherent elasticity of general principles is limited by the conservative approach of the courts to the extension of liability. Systematic development, practical convenience and justice require controlled growth. Nonetheless, courts have not hesitated to extend liability where legal or public policy so requires. One can discern a strong evolutionary trend in judgments since the mid-1970s and the Bill of Rights has already had a significant impact. Courts are evolving new or modified legal principles, which lay the foundation for further ad hoc policy decisions influenced by the particular facts of each case. A general criterion of reasonableness, based upon public policy, the legal convictions of the community, orboni mores, now plays a dominant role in fixing and limiting liability, and has replaced the traditional focus on foreseeability of harm. The tests for wrongfulness and legal causation, in particular, have a strong policy base, but these are not the only instances where policy decisions are made. Policy also dictates whether a delictual action is available, whether liability should be strict or based upon fault, whether someone has title to sue, what form intention should take, what constitutes negligent conduct, what constitutes actionable harm and who should bear the onus of proof and the extent of such onus.

The law of delict still has a strong, individualistic character. In effecting a compromise between conflicting interests, the interests of the particular individuals involved are primarily taken into account. The basic approach to allocating liability for harm caused revolves around the question of which of the two individuals concerned (actor or victim) must bear the loss. The loss is shifted to the actor by means of liability only if he or she has culpably infringed the rights of the victim; otherwise, the loss lies where it falls (casum sentit dominus; res perit domino). How this is done, is discussed in the next rubric.

36. The individualistic character of the law of delict is also apparent from the entrenchment of the fault principle in theory and practice. In principle, loss caused by wrongful conduct is compensated by the actor only if he or she was at fault; in the case of the infringement of interests of personality, intent (dolus) is required, and in the case of pecuniary harm at least negligence (culpa) must be proved. In general, therefore the principle of no liability without fault is still of fundamental importance to South African law.

'Social interest is not ignored, however. As indicated above, public policy plays an important role in the loss allocation process and the test for wrongfulness is often expressed in the form of the demands of the boni mores, or the legal convictions, of society. Public interest would also account for the development of no-fault liability'

It is clear in the discussion in LAWSA that this is directly applicable in the South-African sports law.

If a player, player A, contravenes the rules of the game and another player, player B, suffers damage, then Player B would be able to claim compensation for the damages suffered from Player A.

The elements of a delict are the following: An Act, wrongfulness, dolus, causal link between damages and act, damages.

If the above-mentioned elements are present then a person, whether in sport or not, may claim damages from another person.

§5. Contract

37. I am not going to waste the readers' time by discussing in full the history of the South-African contract law. I will, however, mention that the English doctrine of consideration forms no part of the South-African contractual law. This was the case since 1919 when the appellate division held the following in *Conradie v. Rossouw* 1919 AD 279: 'According to our law, if two or more persons, of sound mind and capable of contracting, enter into a lawful agreement, a valid contract arises between them enforceable by action. The agreement may be for the benefit of one of them or of both (Grotius at 3.6.2). The promise must have been made with the intention that it should be accepted (Grotius at 3.1.48); according to Voet, the agreement must have been entered into serio ac deliberato animo. And this is what is meant by saying that the only element that our law requires for a valid contract is consensus, naturally within proper limits – it should be in or de re licita ac honesta.'

The South-African contract law is still based on the above principle.

The facts speak for itself that this is directly relevant to the sports law in South-Africa.

With the entertainment value growing the contracts that players are signing and entertainment contracts with regards to the media rights etc. is growing at an enormous rate.

Sports law does have certain terms that are in my opinion unique to this kind of law. The terms that I am referring to are terms such as game bonuses as well as winning bonuses.

These terms are based on a type of a *'performance bonus'* the player will only get compensation if he plays the game or if the team wins etc. Therefore, this type of compensation is not fully within the hands of the player. He cannot decide if he would be selected for the team on a particular date or that he would not be injured and so on and so forth.

These terms are in my opinion sui generis in nature as the player's performance in terms of the contract is not solely within his own hands.

§6. Criminal Liability

38. The South-African criminal law is regulated by statute as well as common law. Criminal law is the law that determines the punishment for offences and crimes committed by them.

Examples of statutory offences are:

- the income tax acts;
- traffic laws; and
- contravention of the exchange control act.

Examples of common law criminal offences are:

- murder;
- culpable homicide;
- theft;
- robbery;
- assault; and
- fraud.

39. The above examples are not conclusive lists. It is mentioned for explanational purposes.

As mentioned earlier, a person can be liable on a civil as well as a criminal level for the same misconduct.

Say for instance a player gets assaulted by another player, and player B suffers damages as a result of said assault.

Player B would then be able to lay a criminal charge against player A for the assault as well as claim the damages suffered.

The South-African law system requires a different measure of the burden of proof in criminal and in civil litigation. In civil matters, the burden of proof would be on a balance of probabilities.

In criminal matters, as a result of the presumption of innocence, the burden of proof is one of the above reasonable doubts. This means that if there exists a shred of doubt whether or not a person committed a crime the person must be acquitted of said crime.

Criminal conduct is normally accompanied by a culpable state of mind, *mens rea,* and is generally intentional but is not necessarily so in respect of that conduct where statutory law absolutely prohibits the doing of an act and makes it an offence without the reference to the state of mind of the offender. Also in respect of one common law offence, *viz* culpable homicide, it is not necessary that there be an intent, it suffices if the offender acted negligently.

In the South-African system, we have judges as well as magistrates. The magistrates would preside over the so-called minor misconduct cases, 'smaller cases', and the Judges would preside over the more serious cases. The judges are the presiding officers in the High Court of the Republic of South-Africa, and magistrates preside in the Magistrates' court.

It is possible for magistrates as well as judges to hear criminal as well as civil cases.

It is in the interest of justice and of the public that players on the field will not be given a free ticket to do anything they see fit when they are on the playing field.

§7. Liability: Sports Injuries

40. It is possible in South-Africa to obtain legal liability with reference to an injury which injury occurred during the practice of sport.

Injuries in contact sports are almost inevitable and would normally not result in legal action as the sports were played by way of an consensual agreement and with the consciousness of mind that an injury is more reasonable to occur.

For an injury to result in any legal dispute, criminal or civil, it must have been the result of an unlawful action.

The law of delict makes provision that an injured player or spectator is able to claim compensation for physical, psychological and financial damage caused by an injury that was committed negligently or intentionally by another player or official.

The above harm must be caused by the unlawful and culpable act of another person. The last-mentioned person would then be liable on the ground of delict.

I am not going to discuss the elements of a delictual act again as it was already discussed previously herein. I am going to discuss the liability for sports injuries with reference to specific sports in the paragraphs following:

I. Boxing and Wrestling

41. Boxing and wrestling are lawful sports and the participants are immune from both criminal and civil actions despite serious and even potentially fatal injuries that can be inflicted. Both these sports are regulated in South-Africa Boxing and Wrestling Control Act.[40] This act was amended numerous times with the last amendment in 2001 as quoted above.

The Courts have summed up the unlawful sports as sports that have the aim to inflict injury and a motive of personal animosity. It was found in the *Supreme Court of Victoria in Pallante v. Stadiums property Limited* (No. 1) that, I quote,: '... not an unlawful and criminal activity so long as, whether for reward or not, it was conducted by a contestant as a boxing sport or contest, not from the motive of personal animosity, or at all events not predominantly from that motive, but predominantly

40. Boxing and wrestling Control Act, 39 of 1954.

as an exercise of boxing skill and physical condition in accordance with rules and in conditions the object of which was to ensure that the infliction of boxing harm was kept within reasonable bounds, so as to preclude or reduce, so far as is practicable, the risk of either contestant incurring serious head injury, and to ensure that victory should be achieved in accordance with rules by demonstrating the greater skill as a boxer'.

Boxing or wrestling is thus not unlawful. Therefore, the injury inflicting in a boxing contest would be considered as justifiable on the ground of consent as long as it happened within the rules of the sport.

Even though one can mention numerous contact sports that are as dangerous, may be more dangerous than boxing, it would be considered as being lawful of the dominant object of the sport is competition and not in infliction of injury, and provided that the sport does not involve a breach of the peace, the Courts in South-Africa would most probably consider it as lawful.

In the aforementioned, it is clear that in boxing, no participant would be legally liable for an act that was within the rules of the sport.

II. Golf

42. Even though golf is considered to be a non-contact sport, bad shots or negligent acts by the participants can lead to serious injury to other players, but more likely to spectators.

Golf clubs and balls are objects that can cause serious harm. Reasonable care should be exercised in every situation. Negligence is a failure to conform to the standard of reasonable care. A bad shot would not be considered negligent even though it was reasonably foreseeable. It forms part of the sport. There is however an obvious duty of care that rests upon the player; he must aim as accurately as possible and address the ball as good as possible.

It would furthermore be expected that the player should look out and try to avoid injury to any person in the vicinity where the ball is expected to land.

It would be considered gross negligence if the player is so angry and frustrated, at himself for hitting a bad shot that he throws and/or swings his golf club. If he makes contact with another person by doing that, he would be criminally as well as delictually liable for the harm caused to the other person.

III. Soccer

43. Again as explained previously, infractions of the rules of the game resulting in injury might incur liability.

There are a few rules that came into existence in attempt to limit the injuries. In most cases, if the injury that a player suffered is not of a serious nature, there will be no prosecution outside of the disciplinary action taken by the various sports bodies. The Disciplinary proceedings would normally be considered sufficient.

IV. Rugby Football

44. As a contact, sport injuries in rugby are bound to occur by the very nature of the game. However, a player causing injury by acting contrary to the rules and usages of the game, intentionally or negligently, may be held liable for damages.

It would be considered negligent for a match official to proceed with a match while all of the rules relating to the safety and age of the player have not been complied with. If harm occurs as a result of this non-compliance, the match official would be liable for the damage caused.

If a player acts in such a way that he makes himself guilty, whether with intent or negligently, of an offence and such offence is the cause of an injury to another person, the player may obtain liability for the damages caused.

V. Cricket

45. More or less like golf, cricket is considered to be a non-contact sport; therefore, injuries are less likely to occur within the context of the game.

But like other sports, there exists a possibility for a person to be held liable for damages caused by another person.

If a player's act intentionally or negligently results in injury, he may be held liable for the damages caused, keeping in mind that the act must be unlawful.

For example, if a player throws his bat out of anger and the bat makes contact with another person resulting in injury, the player would be liable for damages.

In one particular instance,[41] the person played cricket during school under the supervision of a teacher using a cricket stump as a bat. The cricket stump made contact with another scholar's head resulting in injury. The school was held liable for damages suffered as it was deemed negligent for the teacher to allow the children to play with the stump without a metal tip. The teacher acted within the course and scope of his employment, therefore vicarious liability came into play.

VI. Liability of Match Officials and Administrators Negligence

46. It is clear that negligence is more or less the most common principal to consider in determining whether or not a person would be held accountable for damages suffered by another.

In the South-African law, principal of negligence is determined by following the so-called foreseeability test. The test compromises of three elements. I would discuss these three elements in more detail in the paragraphs following:

(1) Would the reasonable person in the proverbial shoes of the actor have foreseen that the Act can cause damage to another person?
(2) Would the reasonable person have taken precautionary measures to prevent harm being inflicted on others?

41. *Broom and Another v. The Administrator*, NATAL* [1966] 1 All SA 52 (D).

(3) Did the person take last-mentioned steps?

In concluding whether or not the person was negligent, a value judgment balancing the above-mentioned elements must be reached:

(1) The reasonable foreseeability depends on external circumstances of a particular situation, the qualities that can be attributed to the reasonable person as well as legal meaning that can be attached to the reasonable foreseeability of the possibility of harm to another.

The foreseeability cannot be found upon statistics or mathematical calculations but is a legal evaluation of risk creation in a certain situation.

Statistics and mathematical calculations will however assist the court in making the legal evaluation as described above.

(2) If the answer to part (1) hereof is affirmative, then the question would arise whether or not a reasonable person would have taken precautionary measures to prevent harm inflicted on other.

This is for instance the 'net' around the discus ring. The net is there in an attempt to prevent the discus from hitting somebody outside of the line of throw.

There are numerous such examples within the sports law.

In South-Africa, security guards are stationed on the side – lines of any big sporting event in order to prevent the crowd storming on to the pitch and injuring the players or even each other.

It is reasonably foreseeable that a person may get hurt within the line of scrummage in a rugby union match; therefore, there are a lot of safety measures in place for this part of the game.

If one follows everything, the chances for being considered negligence would minimalize.

(3) The third question that one would need to answer is whether or not these steps were taken. If all of the 'might be' possible steps to prevent the injury was taken, then a person cannot be considered as being negligent and would therefore not be held liable for the damages suffered by the injured player.

Negligence is determined by applying the aforementioned measures, and the athlete/spectator can only be held liable if it is determined that he/she was negligent in their actions.

§8. Tax

47. The sports industry has recently grown into a force within the legislative field to be reckoned with and is therefore in need of the necessary administrative guidance. This resulted in a separate identifiable body of tax law which is based on the sports industry.

Within the sports law field, certain topics arose which needed the necessary guidance such as, but not exclusively limited to, image rights, player transfers, foreign sportspersons, the tax treatment of sports academies etc.

The Income Tax Act, Act No. 58 of 1962 section 47A–47K makes special provision for sportspersons. The mentioned articles lay down a flat rate of 15% that would be applicable to any amount received by a non-resident entertainer or sportsperson for activities exercised in South-Africa.

The South-African resident that is liable to pay the non-resident sportsperson must withhold 15% of the amount payable for tax purposes.

48. For easy reference, I quote these sections in whole here:

47A. Definitions.– For purposes of this Part–

(a) 'entertainer or sportsperson' includes any person who for reward–
   (i) performs any activity as a theatre, motion picture, radio or television artiste or a musician;
   (ii) takes part in any type of sport; or
   (iii) takes part in any other activity which is usually regarded as of an entertainment character;

(b) 'specified activity' means any personal activity exercised in the Republic or to be exercised by a person as an entertainer or sportsperson, whether alone or with any other person or persons.

47B. Imposition of tax.– (1) Subject to subsection (3), there must be levied and paid for the benefit of the National Revenue Fund a tax, to be known as the tax on foreign entertainers and sportspersons, in respect of any amount received by or accrued to any person who is not a resident (in this Part referred to as the 'taxpayer') in respect of any specified activity exercised or to be exercised by that person or any other person who is not a resident.

(2) The tax on foreign entertainers and sportspersons is a final tax and is levied at a rate of 15% on all amounts received by or accrued to a taxpayer as contemplated in subsection (1).

(3) Subsection (1) does not apply in respect of any person who is not a resident, if that person–
   a. is an employee of an employer who is a resident; and
   b. is physically present in the Republic for a period or periods exceeding 183 full days in aggregate during any 12 month period commencing or ending during the year of assessment in which the specified activity is exercised.

47C. Liability for payment of tax.–(1) A taxpayer must, within 30 days (or within such further period as the Commissioner may approve) after an amount contemplated in section 47B is received by or accrues to that taxpayer, pay to the Commissioner the amount of tax which is leviable in terms of this Part in respect of that amount.

(2) This section does not apply to any amounts received by or accrued to the taxpayer–
   a. from which the full amount of tax has been withheld by a resident in terms of section 47D; or

b. which have been recovered from a resident who is personally liable for the amount in terms of section 47G (1).

47D. Withholding of amounts of tax.–(1) Any resident who is liable to pay to a taxpayer any amount contemplated in section 47B (1)must deduct or withhold from that payment the amount of tax for which the taxpayer is liable under that section in respect of that amount.

(2) A taxpayer from whom an amount has been deducted or withheld in terms of this section is deemed to have received the amount so deducted or withheld.

47E. Payment of amounts of tax deducted or withheld.–(1) A resident must pay any amount deducted or withheld in terms of section 47D to the Commissioner before the end of the month following the month during which that amount was so deducted or withheld.

(2) The payment contemplated in subsection (1) is a payment made on behalf of the taxpayer in respect of his or her liability under section 47B.

47F. Submission of return.–(1) A taxpayer must, together with the payment contemplated in section 47C (1), submit to the Commissioner a return.

(2) A resident who pays to the Commissioner any amount in terms of section 47E, must together with that payment submit to the Commissioner a return.

47G. Personal liability of resident.–(1) A resident who–

a. fails to deduct or withhold an amount of tax in terms of section 47D from any payment made to a taxpayer; or
b. deducts or withholds an amount of tax but fails to pay that amount over in terms of section 47E, is personally liable for payment of that amount of tax in accordance with Part A of Chapter 10 of the Tax Administration Act.

47K. Notification of specified activity.–Any resident who is primarily responsible for founding, organising, or facilitating a specified activity in the Republic and who will be rewarded directly or indirectly for that function of founding, organising or facilitating must, in the manner and form prescribed by the Commissioner–

a. notify the Commissioner of that specified activity within 14 days after the agreement relating to that founding, organising or facilitating of that specified activity has been concluded; and
b. provide to the Commissioner such other details relating thereto as may be required by the Commissioner.

The aforementioned is only applicable on foreign sportspersons or entertainers as can be gathered from section 47B thereof. The South-African sportsperson's tax, who is a resident of South-Africa, would be calculated by way of the normal South-African tax calculations that is applicable to any other employee that is employed by an South-African employer.

The governance of the employer, employee relationship will be more fully discussed in the following chapter.

Part II. Sport and Employment

Chapter 1. General Issues

§1. Amateur and Professional Participation in Sport

49. Before I deal with the sport and employment issues, it is important to first discuss the amateur and professional legs of sport in South-Africa.

South-Africa is a country that is particularly fond of sport and does have a huge amateur leg of sport.

Most of the Schools in the country offer a variety of sports for the learners to participate in, the most common of which is rugby, netball, cricket, football, tennis etc.

These amateur legs of South-African sports are governed by the rules and regulations of the different sporting associations.

The professional leg is a bit more complex in the sense that it would not anymore only involve the rules and regulations of the particular sport. The employee and employer relationship situation and the acts governing same would then come into play.

§2. Sport & Employment

50. Contracts between the player and the owners of the teams they compete in can be an employment contract or a contract to render a specific service. In terms of the contract law in South-Africa and the right to conclude a contract, the latter-mentioned contract will more or less be solely determined by the terms thereof.

If an employment contract is concluded between the player and the owners of the association he is playing for, the statutes that deal with employment relations would be applicable. The most important of these statutes are the following:

- The Labour Relations Act;[42] ('LRA')
- The Basic Conditions of Employment Act;[43] (TBCEA)
- The Employment Equity Act;[44]
- The Promotion of Equality and Unfair Discrimination Act;[45]

42. Act 66 of 1995.
43. Act 75 of 1997.
44. Act 55 of 1998.
45. Act 4 of 2000.

- The Unemployment Insurance Act;[46]
- The Occupational Health and Safety Act;[47]
- The Occupational Injuries and Diseases Act;[48]
- The Skills Development Act.[49]

51. The most important of the aforementioned statutes would be the LBA and BCEA. These two acts deal specifically with the employment relations of any person employed in South-Africa, which will include sportspersons.

In every employment contract, there will always be more than one role player as a result of the aforementioned statutes. The role players would be the parties involved and the state.

In the South-African law, there exist numerous methods to regulate an employment relationship. ADR is the most common method with regards to the sport law and can be implemented in one of the following ways:

- The collective bargaining councils – which will include the CCMA.
- In certain matters the civil courts.
- If it is solely based on a labour dispute the Labour Court would have the necessary jurisdiction.

I. The Labour Relations Act

52. The Labour Relations Act is the vessel in terms of which the doctrine against unfair labour practices is regulated. This act determines guidelines in terms of which each employer-employee must function.

As this is only an oversight of the sports law in South-Africa, I am not going to go into the detail with regards to the procedure of referring a dispute to a bargaining council.

II. The Basic Conditions of Employment Act

53. The minimum terms of an employment contract are determined by the BCEA. The employer is bound by these minimum requirements, but the employer/employee may conclude the employment contract at a better level than the prescribed minimum.

That is, this Act limits the working hours for most employees to 45 hours a week with the exclusion of overtime. Overtime is limited to 3 hours per day and 10 hours per week and must be paid at a minimum rate of 1.5 times the employees' normal hourly rate.

46. Act 63 of 2001.
47. Act 85 of 1993.
48. Act 103 of 1993.
49. Act 97 of 1998.

This Act further determines the minimum leave within the different categories of leave the employee may be entitled to. The different categories of leave referred to are, for example annual, sick, family, responsibility, occasional and maternity leave.

A further important aspect this Act prescribes is the minimum notice period for the termination of the employees' contract of employment.

In terms of this Act, an employer is obliged to give a notice of termination to an employee of not less than:

(1) one week if the employee is employed for less than six months;
(2) two weeks if the employee is employed more than six months but less than a year;
(3) four weeks if the employee:
   - has been employed for one year or more; or
   - is a farm worker or domestic worker who has been employed for more than six months.

54. The above periods may be varied in the event of any cause determined by law.

Employers are further obliged to issue codes of good conduct with regards to working hours, maternity leave and codes of good practice.

Any agreement concluded between an employer and employee may not reduce the leave as determined by the Act; it may furthermore not reduce the employee's rights as provided by this Act. This Act provides a wide discretion to the employer as long as it is reasonable and do not reduce the rights of an employee as determined by this Act.

III. The Employment Equity Act

55. This Act is an important cornerstone with reference to the South-African checkered past. Like the South-African constitution, this Act prohibits unfair discrimination against employees and compels designated employers to develop and implement employment equity plans.

The above-mentioned discrimination can be direct or indirect. It would, for instance, be indirect discrimination based on a specific racial group if the job specification is of such a nature that only one racial group or sex would qualify. Due to the fact that these employment equity plans are implemented to favour the previously disadvantaged groups, it is seen as fair discrimination on racial grounds.

The above is discussed within the context of sports law by way of the discussion by Adv. Anton Alberts on his piece on the quota systems in the Republic of South-Africa for which I sincerely thank him.

A further relevant part of the above-mentioned Act is the fact that it regulates the medical and psychological testing in a certain way.

Medical testing is prohibited unless legislation permits and/or requires the testing. It is also allowed if it is justifiable in light of medical facts, employment conditions, social policy, the fair distribution of employee benefits or the inherent requirements of a job.

The above is the reason why the blood testing of athletes would always be allowed.

§3. AGENTS AND INTERMEDIARIES

56. 'The law of principal and agent governs the relationship between professional sportspersons their agents or managers and the other contracting party (e.g., owners of a club or team). Provided the agent/manager acts within the scope of the mandate of the principal (the player), the latter will be bound by any agreement entered into on his or her behalf, including a contact of employment.'[50]

The above definition is a simple explanation of how the contracts with a sport agent would be determined. The specific intermediary/agent contract would further be governed by regulations of the sport in question and its constitution.

I. Football

57. The South-African football Association (SAFA) adopted the newly introduced FIFA regulations of FIFA as is and would implement it in such a way.

This is discussed in detail by Mrs Wafeekah Begg, the Legal advisor of SAFA in the paragraphs following:

II. Intermediaries in South-Africa

Wafeekah Begg

58. On the 10/11 June 2014, the FIFA Congress adopted a resolution to replace the then existing Players' Agents Regulations with a new regulation titled Regulations on *Working with Intermediaries* in order to 'maintain the integrity of the sport of football by promoting and safeguarding considerably high ethical standards in the relations between players, clubs and third parties, and thus live up to good governance and financial responsibility principles'.

FIFA, therefore, directed that each federation develop its own regulations to comply with its regulations that will have worldwide effect. In response, the South African Football Association's National Executive Committee approved the attached Regulations on Working with Intermediaries at its ordinary meeting held on Friday, 27 March 2015.

59. The system whereby Players' Agents were registered and accredited by the Association has been repealed and all Players' Agents licenses were revoked. Former Players' Agents were expected to return their license cards to the SAFA National Office. However, they have failed to do so. Most of the former licensed

50. J.A.A. Basson & M.M Loubscher, *Sport and the Law in South-Africa* (Butterworths 2000).

Players' Agents formed a voluntary association named South African Football Intermediary Association (SAFIA). SAFIA instituted legal proceedings against the Association seeking to set aside the new SAFA Regulations on Working with Intermediaries. Their main issue of contention in their interdict application was that intermediaries cannot survive financially if their commissions were slashed from 10% to 3%. A reduction in earnings would result in their businesses being forced to close down and thus considered unlawful. The High Court suspended the SAFA Intermediary Regulations pending the review and in the interim the existing SAFA Regulations on Players Agents as approved by the SAFA NEC in August 2012.

The Association then again invited a number of different intermediaries and/or groups representing intermediaries, and/or other stakeholders to make submissions to the Associations Legal and Constitutional Committee of SAFA. In addition to the representations that had already been made, further representations were made by SAFIA and the South African Football Players Union (SAFPU) to the Legal and Constitutional Committee on 13 November 2015.

The Committee took both Associations' presentations and comments into account (together with the prior representations by various interested parties) and put forth a proposal to the SAFA National Executive Committee for consideration and approval.

The SAFA National Executive Committee held its scheduled meeting on Friday, 11 December 2015 and approved certain amendments to the SAFA Regulations on Working with Intermediaries.

The Regulations initially implemented for the 1 April 2015 have been revised, amended and approved by the NEC on the 2 April 2016 and have now come into effect. The revised Regulations focus specifically on registration of the transactions that are concluded, as opposed to licensing of individuals.

III. Registration of a Transaction

60. The Association has implemented the FIFA TMS Intermediary Regulation Tool (IRT) which is designed to facilitate compliance with the Regulations on Working with Intermediaries. All Intermediaries who are engaged in transactions involving players and clubs in their jurisdiction must be registered on the IRT system through the clubs belonging to the Premier Soccer League and National First Division. The IRT system is integrated into the existing FIFA Transfer Matching System (ITMS and DTMS), thus allowing the transfer of professional players and related Intermediary involvement to be managed via one system.

On the 19 May 2016, the Association held an Intermediaries Regulations and IRT Workshop for the TMS Club Managers to demonstrate the use of the IRT System and explanation of the Regulations on Working with Intermediaries. The information to be submitted to the engaging club includes:

- All agreed remunerations or payments that have been made or are to be made to an Intermediary.
- Intermediary Declaration form A or B (whichever is applicable).
- Intermediary Representation Agreement.

- The necessary consents and declarations about conflict of interest for all involved intermediaries as defined by the Regulations.
- The transfer agreement between the clubs.
- The new employment contract of the player (which must mention the Intermediary and contain his/her signature).

61. Given the legal action brought against the Association, FIFA had granted the Association an extension of six months from 30 March 2016 to publish its first intermediary report in accordance with Article 6.3 of the FIFA Regulations on Working with Intermediaries. The Association has now used the IRT system for the first time in the transfer window period between 1 July 2016 and 31 August 2016. The Association awaits feedback from the clubs in response to their experiences under the Regulations on Working with Intermediaries and the application of the IRT System.

IV. Rugby

62. The player's agent's regulations were adopted at a general meeting on 1 April 2016. These regulations determine the manner in which the board would be compiled and the term the members may serve.

The regulations further more determine the disciplinary measures and how they should be implemented.

With regards to the agents, it determines the following:

> Before an agent can be accredited the person must meet all the requirements as set out in the regulations.

63. In terms of clause 4 of the regulations, a person is eligible to become an agent if the following criteria are met, I quote:

> ***1 Eligibility***
> Unless otherwise determined by the Board, in order to be granted and to maintain Accreditation, an Agent must:
> 1.1 satisfy all eligibility criteria in accordance with the Regulations and the SubRegulations as at the time of applying for Accreditation;
> 1.2 be eighteen (18) years or older;
> 1.3 not make any false or misleading statements of a material nature in the application for Accreditation;
> 1.4 not subject him- or herself to the Regulations, the Sub-Regulations or any amendments thereto;
> 1.5 not have a pending criminal charge(s) or have been convicted of any criminal offence (except traffic offences) or been a defendant in any civil proceedings in which a final judgment was made against the Agent involving fraud, forgery, corruption, theft, embezzlement, misappropriation of funds, breach of fiduciary duty, professional negligence or legal malpractice;
> 1.6 not have been disqualified or suspended from any profession;

1.7 not have misappropriated funds, or engaged in other specific acts such as embezzlement, corruption, theft, fraud, bribery or related unlawful activities which would render him/her unfit to serve in a fiduciary capacity on behalf of Players;
1.8 have no previous conviction for legal proceedings brought against the Agent by a Player, Players' Association, SARU, Rugby Body or governing body of a sport;
1.9 have no conflict of interest e.g. the Agent must not be employed, nor be an elected official of a Rugby Body or SARU.
1.10 agree to be subject to and comply with the IRB Bye-Laws and Regulations Relating to Rugby, SARU Constitution, Regulations and Code of Conduct, World Rugby SANZAR Regulations and decisions, including the Agents' Code of Conduct and the Player Agents Regulations in force from time to time.[51]

In terms of clause 12 of the said regulations, practising attorneys (solicitors) or practising advocates are exempted from having to become an accredited agent before dealing as such.

Therefore any practising attorneys with the necessary fidelity fund certificate and a practising advocate who is a member of the national bar society may deal as an agent.

SARPA employees as well as direct family members of the player are also exempted in terms of these regulations.

Before a person may act as an agent, the person must provide the club or interested party with his accreditation card.

In conclusion, it is clear that any person may become a rugby agent if he pays the necessary fees and is eligible in terms of these regulations. He then applies for the accreditation by the board who in turn would take the decision whether or not o issue the person with his accreditation card.

International agents may act as agents in South-Africa if they are registered at their local bodies as agents.

51. The Players' Agents Regulations as accepted on 1 April 2016.

Part III. Doping in Sport

§1. Act 14 of 1997

64. South-Africans as a whole are normally very fond of their sport. As a result hereof, the need to grow bigger and better within the sports field also grow, and to add to this conundrum in the bigger sport, there is a lot of money to be made and therefore more and more athletes tend to medical enhancements that is prohibited.

Doping control in South-Africa has developed immensely since the early 1990s until date. At the University of Free State, there is an accredited WADA registered laboratory. This is one and only in its sort on the African continent.

The South-African institute of drug free sport was established by an Act of Parliament during 1997 – The South-African Institute of Drug-Free Sport Act, Act 14 of 1997.

The last-mentioned act is a short act and I will discuss the said act in the following paragraphs.

§2. The South African Institute for Drug Free Sport

65. The aforementioned act makes provision for the establishment of an institute to regulate and determine the manner in which doping would be curbed.

The motto of the South-African institute for drug-free sport reads as follows:[52]

> The South African Institute for Drug-Free Sport's core focus is to tackle doping in sport in order to ensure a culture of ethics and fair play within South Africa.

We are passionate about sport. And we are passionate about our nation's sporting heroes setting a good example for the younger generation. Not only would we like our athletes to compete drug-free, but we also want them to be proud to say no to doping.

The Drug-Free Sport Act* gives the Institute authority and jurisdiction to carry out drug testing across all sports codes. By doing so, we are inspiring a drug-free sports culture all South-Africans can be proud of.

52. www.drugfreesport.org.za.

66. Their objectives can more or less be summed up as follows:[53]

- To promote participation in sport, free from the use of prohibited substances or methods intended to artificially enhance performance, thereby rendering impermissible doping practices which are contrary to the principles of fair play and medical ethics, in a manner consistent with protecting the health and well-being of competitors, and the rights of all people who take part in sport.
- To encourage the development of programmes for the education of the community in general and the sporting community in particular, in respect of the dangers of doping in sport.
- To provide leadership in the development of a national strategy concerning doping in sport.
- To bring about the introduction of centralized independent sample collection and testing programme, which may subject any sportsperson to dope testing, with or without notice, both in and out of competition.
- To encourage South African national sports federations and other sports organizations to adopt uniform, independent and internationally acceptable sample collection and testing procedures.
- To encourage the development and maintenance of a sport drug testing laboratory or laboratories accredited by the International Olympic Committee.
- To promote and encourage the adoption of uniform sample collection and testing procedures and education programmes relating to doping in sport internationally.

67. The mentioned act works in conjunction with the WADA – world anti-doping code.

The latest version of this code is on WADA's official website.

All of the competing Olympic countries are bound by this code.

In disciplinary hearings of this nature, the onus would rest on the complainant, the sporting body, to prove its case.

One must bear in mind that this is not a trial court and the balance of probabilities would normally prevail as a measure.

Previously rule 59(5) of the IAAF handbook required proof beyond reasonable doubt, but the IAAF has since adopted the WADA code and is also practising within this code.

68. Since its foundation, the Institute:[54]

- Provided leadership in the development of a national anti-doping strategy in sport.
- Developed and implemented a comprehensive drug-testing programme that includes all South Africa's major sporting codes and conforms to the highest international standards of the industry.
- Provided education and information on drugs in sport to all its target markets.

53. AD Loubscher's Sport & The Law *supra.*
54. www.drugfreesport.org.za.

- Consulted to other African countries on building capacity towards developing an anti-doping infrastructure on the continent.
- Collaborated with other national anti-doping agencies throughout the world to achieve international harmonization and improvement of standards and practices in anti-doping.

§3. CAS Hearing of Caster Semenya: A Short Summary

69. Even though the aforementioned case doesn't involve doping in sport it does relate to extraordinarily high levels of testosterone within the aforementioned female athlete's body. The Court for arbitration in sport's decision went against Semenya, but the decision is currently in the appeal process of the Swiss Supreme Federal Court of Appeal.

Here follows a short executive summary of the decision of the court for arbitration in sport as to be found on their website. The panel already summarised their decision, therefore, it would bear no meaning for me to summarize same again:

> "*EXECUTIVE SUMMARY*
> ***Introduction***
>
> 1. *On 30 April 2019, the Court of Arbitration for Sport ("CAS") delivered an Award with respect to the challenges brought by Caster Semenya and Athletics South Africa ("ASA") to the validity of the IAAF's Eligibility Regulations for the Female Classification (Athletes with Differences of Sex Development) (the "DSD Regulations"). By a majority, the CAS Panel dismissed the requests for arbitration considering that the Claimants could not establish that the DSD Regulation were "invalid". The Panel found that the DSD Regulations are discriminatory but that, on the basis of the evidence submitted by the parties, such discrimination is a necessary, reasonable and proportionate means of achieving the legitimate objective of ensuring fair competition in female athletics in certain events and protecting the "protected class" of female athletes in those events. The Panel also expressed serious concerns about the future practical application of the DSD Regulations. While the evidence has not established that those concerns are justified, or that they negate the conclusion of prima facie proportionality, this may change in the future unless constant attention is paid to the fairness of how the Regulations are implemented.*
>
> ***The DSD Regulations***
>
> 2. *In 2014 the Indian athlete Dutee Chand brought proceedings before the CAS challenging the IAAF Regulations Governing Eligibility of Females with Hyperandrogenism to Compete in Women's Competition (the "Hyperandrogenism Regulations"). In July 2015, the CAS delivered an Interim Award partially upholding Ms. Chand's challenge and suspending the Hyperandrogenism Regulations (CAS 2014/A/3759 Dutee Chand v AFI & IAAF).*

3. *In Chand, the CAS had determined that the hormone testosterone was the primary cause for the increase in lean body mass in males at puberty and that this provided athletic advantage to male athletes over female athletes. The Panel in that case was not satisfied as to the degree of that advantage and declined to validate the Hyperandrogenism Regulations. The IAAF was given the opportunity to provide further evidence to validate those regulations, which had set the maximum level of testosterone for an athlete in female competition to 10 nmol/L, this being well above the maximum level in the female population and slightly above the minimum level in the male population.*
4. *In March 2018, the IAAF informed the CAS that it intended to withdraw the Hyperandrogenism Regulations and to replace them with new Regulations.*
5. *In April 2018, the IAAF enacted the DSD Regulations. In summary, the DSD Regulations establish new requirements governing the eligibility of women with certain differences of sex development ("DSD") to participate in the female classification in eight events (the "Restricted Events") at international athletics competitions ("International Competitions"). The Restricted Events include the 400m, 800m and 1500m races – events in which Ms. Semenya regularly participates at International Competitions.*
6. *During the course of the proceedings before the CAS, the IAAF explained that, following an amendment to the DSD Regulations, the DSD covered by the Regulations are limited to "46 XY DSD" – i.e. conditions where the affected individual has XY chromosomes. Accordingly, no individuals with XX chromosomes are subjected to any restrictions or eligibility conditions under the DSD Regulations.*
7. *Athletes with 46 XY DSD have testosterone levels well into the male range. The DSD Regulations require athletes with 46 XY DSD who have a natural testosterone level of above 5 nmol/L, and who experience a "material androgenizing effect" from that enhanced testosterone level, to reduce their natural testosterone level to within the normal female range (i.e. to a level below 5 nmol/L) and to maintain that reduced level for a continuous period of at least six months in order to be eligible to compete in a Restricted Event at an International Competition. There is no requirement for, or suggestion of, any surgical intervention to achieve this level.*

The Claimants' challenges to the validity of the DSD Regulations

8. *The DSD Regulations came into force on 1 November 2018. Prior to that date, however, Ms. Semenya and ASA (collectively, the "Claimants") commenced arbitration proceedings before the CAS challenging the validity of the DSD Regulations.*
9. *The Claimants contended inter alia that the DSD Regulations unfairly discriminate against athletes on the basis of sex and/or gender because they only apply (i) to female athletes; and (ii) to female athletes having certain physiological traits. They submitted that the DSD Regulations lack a sound scientific basis; are unnecessary to ensure fair competition within the*

female classification; and are likely to cause grave, unjustified and irreparable harm to affected female athletes. Accordingly, the Claimants sought an award from the CAS declaring the DSD Regulations unlawful and preventing them from being brought into force on the basis that the Regulations are unfairly discriminatory, arbitrary and disproportionate and therefore violate the IAAF Constitution, the Olympic Charter, the laws of Monaco, the laws of jurisdictions in which international athletics competitions are held, as well as universally recognised fundamental human rights.

10. *In response, the IAAF submitted that the DSD Regulations are based on the best available science; do not discriminate on the basis of any protected characteristic; and are a necessary, reasonable and proportionate means of pursuing the legitimate aim of safeguarding fair competition and protecting the ability of female athletes to compete on a level playing field.*
11. *Between 18-22 February 2019, a hearing of the Claimants' challenges was held before the CAS in Lausanne, Switzerland. The CAS Panel comprised the Hon. Dr. Annabelle Bennett AO SC (President); The Hon. Hugh L. Fraser (Arbitrator) and Dr. Hans Nater (Arbitrator). The Panel received detailed written and oral testimony from a large number of factual and expert witnesses. This included experts specialising in gynaecology, andrology and the causes, diagnosis, effects and treatment of DSD; genetics, endocrinology and pharmacology; exercise physiology and sports performance; medical and research ethics; sports regulation and governance; and statistics.*

The Award of the CAS Panel

12. *After setting out the parties' evidence and submissions, the Panel begins its analysis of the merits by noting that this case involves a complex collision of scientific, ethical and legal conundrums. It also involves incompatible, competing rights. It is not possible to give effect to one set of rights without restricting the other set of rights. Put simply, on one hand is the right of every athlete to compete in sport, to have their legal sex and gender identity respected, and to be free from any form of discrimination. On the other hand, is the right of female athletes, who are relevantly biologically disadvantaged vis-à-vis male athletes, to be able to compete against other female athletes and to achieve the benefits of athletic success. The decision is also constrained by the accepted, necessary, binary division of athletics into male events and female events, when there is no such binary division of athletes. That binary division has not been challenged.*
13. *The Panel has not found the issues in this case easy to decide. It is clear from the range of expert evidence presented on behalf of the parties that there are many scientific, ethical and regulatory issues on which reasonable and informed minds may legitimately differ. The Panel is mindful that, in considering these issues, it is not acting as a policy maker or regulator. It is neither necessary nor appropriate for the Panel to step into the shoes of the IAAF by deciding how it would have approached issues had it been*

charged with making policies or enacting rules itself. Instead, its function is a purely judicial one. The Panel must adjudicate the disputed legal issues on the basis of the applicable legal tests and by reference to the arguments and admissible evidence on the record in these proceedings. While this inevitably requires consideration of arguments and evidence based on an array of policy and scientific matters, the Panel must be mindful of its judicial role and the limits of that role. It is also bound to make its decision based upon the evidence presented to it, taking account of the submissions made by the parties.

Discrimination

14. *The Panel unanimously concludes that the DSD Regulations are prima facie discriminatory since they impose differential treatment based on protected characteristics. In particular, since the DSD Regulations establish restrictions that are targeted at a subset of the female/intersex athlete population, and do not impose any equivalent restrictions on male athletes, it follows that the Regulations are prima facie discriminatory on grounds of legal sex. Similarly, the DSD Regulations create restrictions that are targeted at a group of individuals who have certain immutable biological characteristics (namely a 46 XY DSD coupled with a material androgenising effect arising from that condition), and which do not apply to individuals who do not have those characteristics. It follows that the Regulations are also prima facie discriminatory on grounds of innate biological characteristics.*
15. *The conclusion that the DSD Regulations are prima facie discriminatory is merely the starting point of the Panel's legal analysis. In particular, it is common ground that a rule that imposes differential treatment on the basis of a particular protected characteristic is valid if it is a necessary, reasonable and proportionate means of attaining a legitimate objective.*

Necessity

16. *The majority of the Panel concludes that the IAAF has succeeded in establishing the necessity requirement.*
17. *The Panel begins its consideration of this question by observing that once it is recognised that it is legitimate to have separate categories of male and female competition, it inevitably follows that it is necessary to devise an objective, fair and effective means of determining which individuals may, and which may not, participate in those categories.*
18. *The Panel accepts the IAAF's submission that reference to a person's legal sex alone may not always constitute a fair and effective means of making that determination. This is because the reason for the separation between male and female categories in competitive athletics is ultimately founded on biology rather than legal status. The purpose of having separate categories is to protect a class of individuals who lack certain insuperable performance advantages from having to compete against individuals who*

possess those insuperable advantages. In this regard, the fact that a person is recognised in law as a woman and identifies as a woman does not necessarily mean that they lack those insuperable performance advantages associated with certain biological traits that predominate in individuals who are generally (but not always) recognised in law as males and self-identify as males. It is human biology, not legal status or gender identity, that ultimately determines which individuals possess the physical traits which give rise to that insuperable advantage and which do not.

19. *Accordingly, the purpose of the male-female divide in competitive athletics is not to protect athletes with a female legal sex from having to compete against athletes with a male legal sex. Nor is it to protect athletes with a female gender identity from having to compete against athletes with a male gender identity. Rather, it is to protect individuals whose bodies have developed in a certain way following puberty from having to compete against individuals who, by virtue of their bodies having developed in a different way following puberty, possess certain physical traits that create such a significant performance advantage that fair competition between the two groups is not possible. In most cases, the former group comprises individuals with a female legal sex and a female gender identity, while the latter group comprises individuals with a male legal sex and male gender identity. However, this is not true of all cases. Natural human biology does not map perfectly onto legal status and gender identity. The imperfect alignment between nature, law and identity is what gives rise to the conundrum at the heart of this case.*
20. *The Panel considers that, once it is recognised that the reason for organising competitive athletics into separate male and female categories rests on the need to protect one group of individuals against having to compete against individuals who possess certain insuperable performance advantages derived from biology rather than legal status, it follows that it may be legitimate to regulate the right to participate in the female category by reference to those biological factors rather than legal status alone.*
21. *It was common ground between the parties that there is a substantial difference in elite sports performance between males and females. It was also common ground that (a) the normal female range of serum testosterone, produced mainly in the ovaries and adrenal glands, is 0.06 to 1.68 nmol/L; and (b) the normal male range of serum testosterone concentration, produced mainly in the testes, is 7.7 to 29.4 nmol/L. On the basis of the scientific evidence presented by the parties, the Panel unanimously finds that endogenous testosterone is the primary driver of the sex difference in sports performance between males and females.*
22. *The IAAF submitted that all but one of the many different factors that contribute to sport performance - including training, coaching, nutrition and medical support, as well as many genetic variations - are equally available to men and women. The only factor that is available only to men is exposure to adult male testosterone levels. The IAAF submitted that if the purpose of the female category is to prevent athletes who lack that testosterone-derived advantage from having to compete against athletes*

who possess that testosterone-derived advantage, then it is necessarily "category defeating" to permit any individuals who possess that testosterone-derived advantage to compete in that category. The majority of the Panel accepts the logic of the IAAF's submission.

23. *Having carefully considered the expert evidence, the majority of the Panel concludes that androgen sensitive female athletes with 46 XY DSD enjoy a significant performance advantage over other female athletes without such DSD, and that this advantage is attributable to their exposure to levels of circulating testosterone in the normal adult male range, rather than the normal adult female range. The majority of the Panel observes that the evidence concerning the performances and statistical over-representation of female athletes with 46 XY DSD in certain Relevant Events demonstrates that the elevated testosterone levels that such athletes possess creates a significant and often determinative performance advantage over other female athletes who do not have a 46 XY DSD condition.*
24. *On this basis, the majority of the Panel accepts that the IAAF has discharged its burden of establishing that regulations governing the ability of female athletes with 46XY DSD to participate in certain events are necessary to maintain fair competition in female athletics by ensuring that female athletes who do not enjoy the significant performance advantage caused by exposure to levels of circulating testosterone in the adult male range do not have to compete against female athletes who do enjoy that performance advantage.*

Proportionality

25. *The majority of the Panel concludes that, on the evidence adduced, the DSD Regulations are on their face reasonable and proportionate. In reaching this conclusion, the majority notes, amongst other things, that the DSD Regulations do not require any athlete to undergo any surgical intervention, and envisage that affected athletes can control their testosterone levels by using conventional oral contraceptives. The majority has also had regard to the possible side effects of such oral contraceptives, to the nature of the examinations that will be undertaken for the purpose of determining whether an athlete has experienced a "material androgenising effect" from their high testosterone levels, and the risk of individuals' medical confidentiality being compromised.*
26. *While the majority concludes that the DSD Regulations are not disproportionate on their face, the Panel highlights its serious concerns about aspects of the practical application of the DSD Regulations when they are implemented. In particular, the Panel expresses its concerns about the potential difficulty for an athlete in complying with the requirements under the Regulations (including the possibility that affected athletes may inadvertently, and through no fault of their own, be unable consistently to maintain a natural testosterone level below 5 nmol/L). The Panel also notes the paucity of evidence to justify the inclusion of two events (the 1500m and one mile events) within the category of Restricted Events. The Panel*

strongly encourages the IAAF to address the Panel's concerns in its implementation of the DSD Regulations. At the same time, the majority of the Panel observes that it may be that, on implementation and with experience, certain factors, supported by evidence, may be shown to affect the overall proportionality of the DSD Regulations, either by indicating that amendments are required in order to ensure that the Regulations are capable of being applied proportionately, or by providing further support for or against the inclusion of particular events within the category of Restricted Events.

The Panel's expression of gratitude to Ms. Semenya

27. *In its Award the Panel expressly pays tribute to Ms. Semenya's grace and fortitude throughout this process. The Panel expresses its profound gratitude for her dignified personal participation and the exemplary manner in which she has conducted herself throughout the proceedings.*
28. *The Panel also stresses that while much of the argument in this proceeding has centred around the "fairness" of permitting Ms. Semenya to compete against other female athletes, there can be no suggestion that Ms. Semenya (or any other female athletes in the same position as Ms. Semenya) has done anything wrong. This is not a case about cheating or wrongdoing of any sort. Ms. Semenya is not accused of breaching any rule. Her participation and success in elite female athletics is entirely beyond reproach and she has done nothing whatsoever to warrant any personal criticism.*

DISCUSSION

Athletics South-Africa, ASA, is very dissatisfied with the aforementioned decision as they are of the opinion that it infringes upon the Semenya's fundamental rights. The condition is not as a result of Semenya's own doing and therefore it would be unfair to expect Semenya to take medication to keep her natural testosterone down.

The aforementioned is also the crux of Semenya's appeal to the Swiss Federal Supreme Court, which appeal is led by Dorothy Schramm of Sidley Austin LLP. She states expressly that "The IAAF regulations violate the most fundamental principles of Swiss public policy. In the race for justice, human rights must win over sporting interests."

Part IV. Sport and Commerce

Chapter 1. General Issues

70. With the huge growth within the sports sector, one concerning issue is that there exists no specific statutory remedy to protect a celebrity's image rights but is this aspect still governed by way of the common law in South-Africa.

The Law of South-Africa vol. 8 (2ed) in paragraph 482 state the following. Actors, musicians, sportspersons and other celebrities are increasingly contracted to market products and services. Such marketing may take the form of the use of, for example, the celebrity's name, image, photograph, likeness or voice.[55] These advertisements may consist of the celebrity actively endorsing or recommending a product. Alternatively, the advertisement may refer to the celebrity's name or image and thus link it to the product. Endorsements usually take place with the consent of the celebrity on a commercial basis, but endorsements occasionally occur without the consent (and sometimes without the knowledge) of the celebrity.[56] Using a person's image, name or likeness without their consent could give rise to a delictual claim for defamation, breach of privacy and, possibly, a breach of the person's right to publicity.

71. The use of a person's image, name or likeness in an advertisement without his or her consent will amount to defamation if it has the effect of reducing the reputation of the person in the eyes of right-thinking members of the public. This may, for example, arise where a person is linked to a product or service which is in some way derogatory in the circumstances,[57] or where the creation of an impression that the person has been paid to endorse a particular product is in itself defamatory.[58]

---

55. T. Woker, *Advertising Law in SA,* 68–69 (Juta 1999).
56. Woker 68–69, 83–84.
57. *See*, e.g., *Plumb v. Jeyes Sanitary Compound Co Ltd The Times* 15 April 1937, discussed in McQuoid-Mason *The Law of Privacy in SA* 209–210. A photograph of a policeman wiping his brow was used to advertise the defendant's product, without the consent of the policeman. The caption to the photograph stated: 'Phew! I am going to get my feet into a Jeye's fluid footbath.' The English court held that the statement contained an innuendo with regard to the condition of the policeman's feet, and that this innuendo was defamatory.
58. For example, in *Tolley v. Fry (JS) & Sons Ltd* 1930 1 KB 467 (HL); 1931 All ER 131 (HL), the House of Lords held that the use of an amateur golfer's image in an advertisement for Fry's chocolate was defamatory as the impression was created that the golfer had consented to a paid endorsement which would imperil his status as an amateur golfer.

The appropriation of another's name or likeness is a recognizable ground for invasion of privacy.[59] This includes the use of a person's name or likeness in an advertisement without that person's consent.[60] Unlike in a claim for defamation, it is not necessary for this action to succeed to prove that the reputation of the plaintiff has been undermined. In *O'Keeffe v. Argus Printing & Publishing Co Ltd*,[61] the court held that '[t]he unauthorised publication of a person's photograph and name for advertising purposes is in my view capable of constituting an aggression upon that person's dignitas'.[62]

72. The requirement of consent for endorsements is emphasized in the provisions of the Code of the Advertising Standards Authority (ASA) of South Africa (the 'code') relating to the protection of privacy and the exploitation of the individual. The code provides that an advertisement should not portray or refer to, by whatever means, any living persons, unless their express prior permission has been obtained.[63] This prohibition, however, does not apply to the following circumstances:

(a) the use of crowd or background shots, provided the portrayal and the context in which it appears is not defamatory, offensive or humiliating;
(b) advertisements for books, films, radio or television programmes, press features and the like, in which there appear portrayals of, or references to, individuals who form part of their subject matter; police or other official notices; and
(c) where, in the opinion of the 'ASA' of South Africa the reference or portrayal is not inconsistent with the individual's right to a reasonable degree of privacy and does not constitute an unjustifiable commercial exploitation of the individual's fame or reputation.

73. In addition, the Sponsorship Code published by the ASA prohibits, as a form of ambush marketing, an organization from using endorsements of athletes, sportspersons, performers or artistes in advertising to create the impression that the organization is connected with the sponsorship of an event, where that organization has no contractual rights to do so. Moreover, athletes, performers or artistes with

59. McQuoid-Mason 208.
60. McQuoid-Mason 208–213.
61. 1954 3 SA 244 (C).
62. At 249D per Watermeyer AJ. In the *O'Keeffe* case, the plaintiff complained that her photograph and name had been used for advertising purposes without her consent. The first defendant was the owner of a newspaper, and the second defendant was the exclusive factory distributor of certain makes of rifles, pistols, revolvers and ammunition. A photograph of the plaintiff, who was an announcer and producer employed by the South African Broadcasting Corporation, was used in the advertisement of the second defendant and was published in the newspaper owned by the first defendant. The court dismissed an exception taken by the defendants that the publication of the advertisement was not capable of constituting an *injuria*. Watermeyer AJ emphasized, however, that not all unauthorized publications of a person's photograph and name for advertising purposes constitute *injuria*. He stated that 'much must depend upon the circumstances of each particular case, the nature of the photograph, the personality of the plaintiff, his station in life, his previous habits with reference to publicity and the like': 249D–E.
63. S II par 11.1 of the code.

individual sponsorship contracts may not, without specific permission from a primary event sponsor, promote their individual sponsor's logo in any way while associated with the primary event sponsor.

Chapter 2. Public Regulations

§1. Media and Television Rights

74. Media and television rights in South-Africa is regulated by the Independent Communications Authority of South Africa (ICASA).

ICASA is the regulator for the South-African communications, broadcasting and postal services sector and is established by the Independent Communications Authority of South-Africa Act, 13 of 2000.[64]

The working of the aforementioned regulator is provided for in the Electronic Communications Act, 13 of 2005 ('ECA').

In terms of section 60(1) and (2) read together with section 4(1) of the ECA the ICASA published Sports Broadcasting services regulations.[65]

These regulations regulate the broadcasting of national sporting events in the republic; it determines the criteria to be used in the listing of the national sporting events and provides a dispute resolution system.

75. In terms of section 5 of the said regulations, the following sporting events would be deemed as national sporting events the Summer Olympic games, The Paralympics, the Commonwealth Games, the All Africa Games, the FIFA world Cup, the Africa cup of nations, the IRB Rugby World Cup, the ICC Cricket World, the ICC T 20 Cricket World Championships, the Comrades Marathon, the Two Oceans Marathon, Super rugby competition, COSAFA CUP, CAF Champions league, CAF Confederations Cup, Telkom Charity cup, MTN Supa 8 Cup, Telkom Knockout, Nedbank Cup, Currie Cup, MTN 40 and the International Boxing Federations.

---

64. Act 13 of 2000.
65. **GNR.275 of 7 April 2010: Sports Broadcasting Services Regulations, 2010** INDEPENDENT COMMUNICATIONS AUTHORITY OF SOUTH AFRICA

2. Object of the regulations.–The object of these regulations is to–

(a) Regulate the broadcasting of national sporting events in the Republic;
(b) Determine the criteria to be used in the listing of national sporting events;
(c) Identify and list national sporting events; and
(d) Provide a dispute resolution mechanism.

3. Scope of regulations.–

(1) These Regulations shall apply to Free-to-air and Subscription broadcasting service licensees.

4. Criteria for identifying national sporting events of public interest.–

(1) The Authority has used the following criteria in determining national sporting events that are of public interest–
(a) a confederation sporting event involving a national team or an individual;
(b) a semi-final and final of a national knockout competition; or
(c) an opening game, semi-final and final of a confederation sporting event.
(2) Any new sporting event that falls within the criteria mentioned in regulation 4 (1) (*a*) – (*c*) above shall be considered for listing during the review period in terms of regulation 7.

As the main sponsor would sometimes change, it is a provision in these regulations that the sporting events as listed would remain national sporting events irrespective of the might be name changes of such events.

It determines further that any of the broadcasting service licensees who enter into a commercial agreement with regards to the broadcasting of the national sporting events must include in that agreement an ADR clause. All the parties to the agreement are bound by this clause, and the arbitration decision would be deemed as final.

§2. Sponsoring

I. Introduction

76. As a result of the large influx of money into sport, it has become an enormous drawing power. Sponsorship[66] as well as broadcasting and advertising rights are some of the major avenues in which more than average income is being generated. Since South-Africa's readmission into the international sporting community, the aforementioned caused a big boom within the market.

It is extremely profitable and rewarding for corporations to associate their products and/or services with certain events, teams or athletes.

On the flip side, the income generated from sponsorships is mostly critical for the team, event, athlete etc. most teams will not survive without the mentioned income.

Accordingly, in recent decades, sponsorship has become an increasingly important part of the sporting industry. Whether it has been at the elite level or closer to the grass-roots level, the search for sponsorship has become vital to the funding and growth of sport. As the significance of sponsorship has grown, the need to understand it and to maximize its potential has greatly increased.

As there exist no statutory requirements in the South-African law system which prescribe the form and/or content of a sponsorship agreement, the general principles of the contract law in South-Africa applies.

II. Sponsors and Sponsorships

77. To accommodating multi-sponsors it has become necessary to develop various types of categories of sponsors. Without these categories, it would be merely impossible to owe up to the demands of the various sponsors.

III. Types of Sponsors

78. The categorization of sponsors has assisted in the maximization of commercial returns for teams and event organizers, and has allowed some commercially

66. E.L. Wood, *Butterworths forms & Precedents, Commercial Transactions*, 1997.

'smaller players' to become involved in sponsoring a team or event without having to make available the same amount of finances as the main sponsor would have to do.

Given the high costs of running a team, the magnitude of some of today's sporting events and the funds required in order to stage events, it is often not possible for a single sponsor alone to provide sufficient funds to run a team or to stage a major event. Accordingly, it is often necessary to involve a number of sponsors. It therefore becomes necessary to categorize sponsors in this 'multi-sponsor environment'. The relationship between various sponsors could be described as either a vertical relationship (where there is a hierarchical relationship between sponsors) or a horizontal relationship (where there is no hierarchical relationship and all sponsors enjoy substantially the same rights and privileges). Of course, a situation can arise (and often does) where one encounters both vertical relationships and horizontal relationships.

It is not common for teams and/or events to be funded by a single sponsor. However, it may be possible to run certain teams, stage smaller events, 'once-off' events or annual events with a single sponsor. This will, of course, depend on the funding requirements of the relevant team or event. It is highly improbable that a major sporting event such as the FIFA Soccer World Cup would survive with just one sponsor or that a major sporting team such as the Manchester United football club could afford its high salary bill with a single sponsor. Then again, there is generally not a shortage of potential sponsors for such events or teams. The various rights and privileges which may arise as a result of being a sole sponsor would be negotiated between the parties and will generally vary depending on the team, the nature of the event, the magnitude of the sponsorship and, of course, the rights which the team or event organizer is willing to confer upon the sponsor where there is a sole sponsorship. Typically, the most important right which may be granted would be the naming rights of the team or event.

Where a team or event needs more than one sponsor, complications may arise and the expectations of the various tiers of sponsors will need to be managed and regulated. In these circumstances, the rights and interests of the sponsors and the team or event organizer will have to be weighed and negotiated as well as the rights of the sponsors *inter se* to avoid any potential conflicting rights being granted. In this regard, the parties may agree to establish a hierarchical level of sponsorship between the sponsors (a vertical relationship). This could be achieved by having a 'main sponsor' or 'title sponsor' with the remaining sponsors falling into a hierarchical chain behind the main or title sponsor and each sponsor enjoying different rights and privileges depending on the magnitude of the sponsorship. For example, the main sponsor may acquire the right to name the event, for example, the 'Coca-Cola Cup' or the 'Vodacom Cup'. Alternatively, the sponsors could enjoy a horizontal relationship *inter se*. This horizontal relationship is often referred to as 'co-sponsorship'.

IV. Types of Sponsorship Agreement

79. There are various types of agreement which may be loosely termed 'sponsorship agreements'. These include:

(a) An agreement whereby one party agrees to make payment to another in consideration for being given publicity in connection with an event or events staged by the second party. In this context, the word 'publicity' must be used in the broad sense and can include advertising rights, broadcast rights etc.
(b) An agreement whereby a party pays a certain amount to or towards certain expenses of a public figure, sporting figures or team in consideration for endorsement by that public figure, sporting figure or team of certain products or services sold or provided by the first party.
(c) An agreement whereby one party, either free or for consideration, provides certain playing or other equipment, products, supplies or services for use by an individual, team or entity in consideration for endorsement by the individual, team or entity of the sponsor's product, supplies and/or services (as the case may be). Such endorsement could take the form of brand association, advertising and/or promotional opportunities. Examples of this type of sponsorship agreement include an official sports drinks sponsor, a clothing sponsor or an official airline sponsor.

80. In addition, a sponsor could be categorized as:

(1) A team sponsor. In that event, the sponsor would sponsor a particular team. A sponsor can sponsor a team for either a fixed period, for example, a season, or for an indefinite period. A sponsor can also sponsor a team for a particular match, event, competition or tournament.
(2) An event sponsor. A sponsor can sponsor an entire event, such as the J & B Met. In this case, the sponsor would sponsor the event itself as opposed to an individual or a team. Depending on the level of sponsorship, an event sponsor could acquire the naming rights, such as the 'Vodacom Super 14'. An event sponsor would generally have the right to decide whether to sponsor the event in future years. Also, the events which could be sponsored may vary from annual events to one-off events, or regular (though not annual) events such as the Olympic Games. An event could also refer to a tournament or a competition. An example of a tournament could be the Commonwealth Games and an example of a competition would be the ABSA Cup.
(3) An individual sponsor. Often sponsors will sponsor an individual sportsperson, in which case the sponsor is often referred to as an 'endorsement sponsor'. This is frequently encountered in relation to the world's top tennis players, for example.

Ambush Marketing

81. Of concern to most sponsors and event organizers alike is the threat of ambush marketing. Ambush marketing occurs when a marketer uses the goodwill and publicity value of a team or an event to obtain a benefit without paying for the right to do so. Ambush marketing draws on the association value of a brand, but in an unauthorized manner without passing on value to the rightful owner of it. Typically, ambush marketing plagues large international events such as the Olympic Games and World Cup events. Ambush marketing is also sometimes referred to as marketing 'by way of intrusion'.

In instances of ambush marketing, the marketer has the objective of using the event as a springboard to promote his, her or its brand or product without incurring the financial and other obligations of a sponsor. Ambush marketing by intrusion may be done by a party, not being an official sponsor, by:

- Placing advertisements for a product and/or service on the outskirts of a stadium at which a sponsored event is taking place. This is sometimes done by flying branded airships over the stadium or placing posters in the neighbourhood around the stadium.
- Running advertisements which make reference to a sponsored sporting event, without suggesting that the advertiser is a sponsor of the event, but doing so by implication.
- Sponsoring an individual participant at an event where the event is sponsored by another party.
- Distributing flyers and/or other memorabilia such as T-shirts and caps in and around the stadium.
- Sponsoring the television broadcast of the event or purchasing considerable airtime during the broadcast of the event.

82. Ambush marketers try to deceive the public into thinking that the ambusher is associated with the event, by using the event's recognized marks and logos, such as the Olympic rings or the International Cricket Council's logo without permission to do so.

Ambush marketing threatens both the integrity and the financial viability of an event, in that official sponsors may in future become reluctant to sponsor an event if they can achieve the same amount of marketing without paying the high sponsorship fees by embarking on ambush-marketing programmes. In addition, it is argued that ambush marketing is an unethical practice. Ambush marketing is prejudicial to both the sponsor and the event organizer in that the event organizer is often dependent upon revenues from sponsorships in order to fund the event. It will be difficult for an event organizer to obtain sponsors in future if it allows ambush marketing to continue. Furthermore, ambush marketing prejudices event sponsors who pay large amounts of money for the privilege of being associated with an event.

In an attempt to prohibit ambush marketing, the Merchandise Marks Act[67] was amended by the Merchandise Marks Amendment Act[68] ('the Amendment Act'). The Amendment Act amended the Merchandise Marks Act by, *inter alia*, inserting the definition of an 'event'. An 'event' is defined as any exhibition, show or competition of a sporting, recreational or entertainment nature which is:

(a) held or to be held in public;
(b) likely to attract the attention of the public or be newsworthy; and
(c) financed or subsidized by commercial sponsorship, and includes any broadcast of such exhibition, show or competition.

83. Further, the Amendment Act provides for the Minister of Trade and Industry, by notice in the Government Gazette, to designate an event as a 'protected event'. Section 15A(2) of the Merchandise Marks Act, as inserted by the Amendment Act, provides that during the period specified in the Government Gazette for which the event is a protected event,[69] no person may use a trademark in relation to such an event in a manner which is calculated to achieve publicity for that trademark and thereby to derive special promotional benefit from the event, without the prior authority of the organizer of such event. For the purpose of section 15A(2), the use of a trademark includes:

(a) any visual representation of the trademark upon or in relation to goods or in relation to the rendering of services;
(b) any audible reproduction of the trademark in relation to goods or the rendering of services; or
(c) the use of the trademark in promotional activities.

Which in any way, directly or indirectly, is intended to be brought into association with or to allude to an event?[70]

In terms of section 15A(4), any person contravening the section will be guilty of an offence. Accordingly, ambush marketing can give rise to criminal sanction and punishment in addition to a possible civil-law claim.

Without derogating from the above, the parties to the sponsorship agreement may themselves take certain steps to prohibit ambush marketing by placing certain obligations on the event organizer to, *inter alia*, ensure that the area around the stadium is 'clean' (in that no competing banners or advertising material will appear in and around the stadium) and further to ensure that no person, not being an official sponsor, will be allowed to advertise or distribute its products within the stadium itself.

'Moral' Rights

---

67. 17 of 1941.
68. 61 of 2002.
69. As to the period for which protection extends, *see* the Merchandise Marks Act 17 of 1941s 15A(1).
70. Act 17 of 1941s 15A(3).

84. It has become common practice for sponsors to attempt to control the use of sponsorship funds by stipulating the exact purpose for which funds provided by them may be used. This is done nowadays so that sponsors know where their funds are being utilized and for what purpose. A sponsor will not want funds provided by it to be utilized to pay bonuses or exorbitant salaries, for example. Rather, the funds should be applied to the running of the team in question or the hosting of the event in question.

In addition, it has become common for sponsors to insist on the right to withdraw from the sponsorship should anything happen which would otherwise damage the reputation of the sponsor in being involved with the team or the event.

Part V. Summary and Specialized Fields in South African Sport

85. With regards to the aforementioned, it deems clear that law in sports is a broad subject and is mostly sui generis in nature due to the fact that it consists of a combination of most of the legal fields.

It has a few peculiarities that you would only find within this field like doping, sponsorship events and/or players, match fees combined with a monthly salary. These are just some of the peculiarities which are explained above.

Sport is the fastest-growing entertainment industry, and there exists a need that this would be recognized as a specialized field of law.

The South-African sports industry is still growing, but it is an extreme force to be reckoned with.

Selected Bibliography

Act 103 of 1993 (s.j.).
Act 17 of 1941 (s.j.).
Act 36 of 2005 (s.j.).
Act 4 of 2000 (s.j.).
Act 61 of 2002 (s.j.).
Act 63 of 2001 (s.j.).
Act 75 of 1997 (s.j.).
Act 85 of 1993 (s.j.).
Act 97 of 1998 (s.j.).
al, G. e., 1998. *Sportslaw.*:
Anon., 1835. Democracy in America.
Anon., s.j. [Kuns].
Anon., s.j.: *http://irr.org.za/reports-and-publications/atLiberty/files/liberty-2013-bee-doesnt-work-but-eed-would.* [Aanlyn].
Anon., s.j. *http://irr.org.za/reports-and-publications/atLiberty/files/liberty-2013-bee -doesnt-work-but-eed-would.* [Aanlyn].
Anon., s.j. *http://mg.co.za/article/2014-09-11-black-players-conflicted-over-new-csa-quotas.* [Aanlyn].
Anon., s.j. *https://www.enca.com/sport/concerns-over-crickets-new-quota-system.* [Aanlyn].
Anon., s.j. *www.drugfreesport.org.za.* [Aanlyn].
Boxing and wrestling Control Act, 39 of 1954. (s.j.).
Boxing and wrestling Control Act, 39 of 1954. (s.j.).
Broad-Based Black Economic Empowerment Act 53 of 2003 (s.j.).
Broom and Another v. The Administrator, Natal (1966 All SA).
Constitution of the Republic of South-Africa, Act 108 of 1996 (s.j.).
Employment Equity Act, 55 of 1998 (s.j.).
Grayson, 1994. *Sport & Law.*
Loabscher, B. &. s.j. *Sport and the Law in South-Africa.*
Midgley & Van Der Walt (s.j.).
National Sport and Recreation Act, 110 of 1998 (s.j.).
Oehly and Others v. Rex 1908 (s.j.).
SARFU and Others v. President of the Republic of South-Africa and Others 1998 (1) BCLR 1256 (T) (s.j.).
Various, s.j. *Law of South Africa.* Vol. 8. 2nd ed. LexisNexis.
Waal, C. &. D., 2005. *Bill of Rights Handbook.* 5th ed.

Selected Bibliography

Index

The numbers here refer to paragraph numbers.

www.ingramcontent.com/pod-product-compliance
Lightning Source LLC
Chambersburg PA
CBHW071358230926
51846CB00002B/587
* 9 7 8 9 4 0 3 5 1 9 4 4 9 *